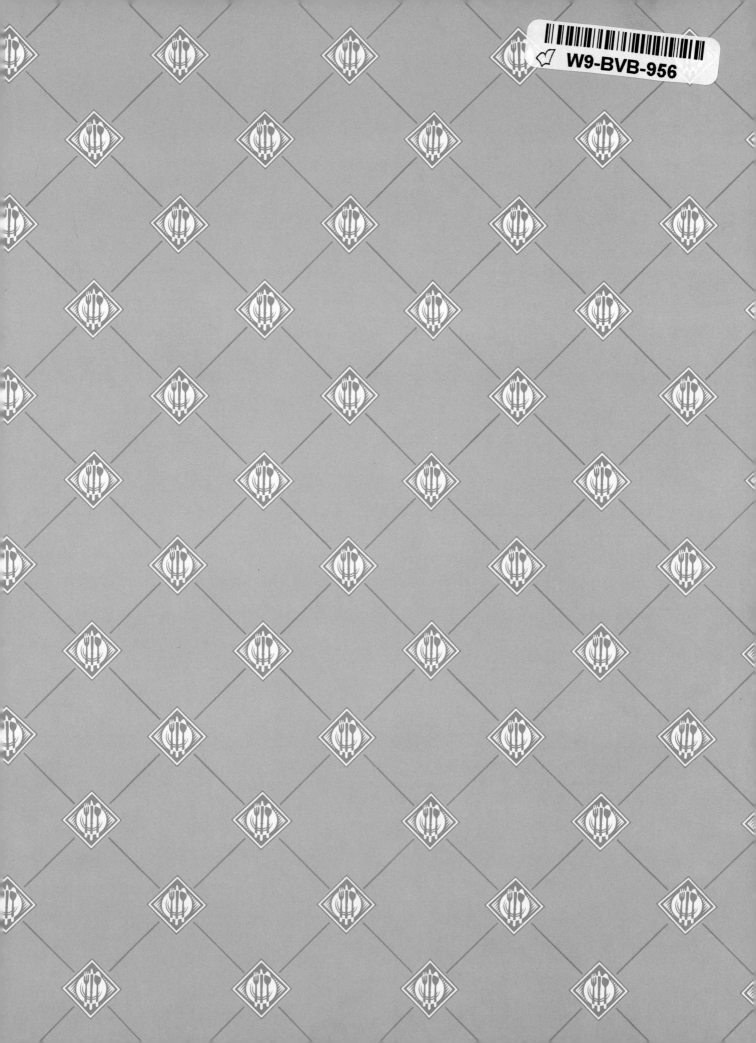

Campbell's

ANNIVERSARY 75th COOKBOOK

Cooking in Minutes

CRESCENT BOOKS

This edition is an enlarged and revised version of the **FAVORITE BRAND NAME RECIPES COOKING IN MINUTES** cookbook.

Copyright © 1991 Campbell Soup Company

"Campbell's" is a registered trademark of Campbell Soup Company.

FAVORITE ALL TIME RECIPES is a trademark of Publications International, Ltd.

This edition was produced by the Publications Center in coordination with Creative Food Center and Communications Center, Campbell Soup Company, Campbell Place, Camden, NJ 08103-1799.

Managing Editor: Pat Teberg
Contributing Editors: Julia Malloy, Patricia A. Ward
Home Economists: Linda Armor, Lisa Miller, Patricia Owens, Margaret Romano
Photographers: William R. Houssell, Nancy Principato, Maggie Wochele
Art Director: Warren Neal
Food Stylist: Patricia A. Ward
Front Cover Food Stylist: Elizabeth J. Barlow
Accessories Stylists: Lee Wilson, Lynn Wilson
Business Manager: Eugene Sung
Public Relations Manager: Kevin Lowery

Pictured on the front cover: Chicken-Broccoli Divan (see recipe, page 9).

Pictured on the back cover: Mini Broccoli Pizzas (see recipe, page 92) and Easy Paella (see recipe, page 54).

ISBN: 1-56173-967-7

This edition was published by:
Publications International, Ltd.
7373 North Cicero Avenue
Lincolnwood, Illinois 60646

8 7 6 5 4 3 2 1

Manufactured in U.S.A

Microwave cooking times in this book are approximate. These recipes have been tested in 650-to 700-watt microwave ovens. Food cooked in lower-wattage ovens may require longer cooking times. Use the cooking times as guidelines and check for doneness before adding more time.

Cooking in Minutes

Quick Cooking With Soup   4
Shortcut cooking tips guaranteed to save you time—

20-Minute Express   8
Souper-fast main dishes ready to eat at a moment's notice—

30-Minute Countdown   26
Beat-the-clock entrées to serve family and friends in just minutes—

Easy-Going Entrées   50
Delicious, hassle-free main dishes ready in less than one hour—

Dishes On The Side   68
A savory selection of easy recipes that round out the meal—

Snacks In A Snap   86
Taste-tempting snacks and appetizers that go together fast—

Food Equivalents Chart   94
Guide of weights and measures for common cooking ingredients—

Index   95

Whether you're busy at home, busy with a career or juggling both, your time for grocery shopping, cooking and cleanup is short. To help you, Campbell's team of experienced home economists has been busy testing and tasting more than 110 timesaving recipes just for you. The result: Campbell's *Cooking in Minutes* cookbook presenting recipes guaranteed to be *M'm! M'm! Good!*

Campbell Soup Company has been giving cooks the kind of recipe ideas and information they've requested for years. Back in 1916, we published one of our first cookbooks, *Helps for the Hostess*, featuring soup as an ingredient in many of the recipes. The cookbook also shared tips on proper table etiquette, napkin folding and menu ideas. But lifestyles have changed. Convenience, taste and value are more important than ever to today's cooks. Campbell's welcomes you to the 1990s with this 75th anniversary soup cookbook full of beat-the-clock recipes, timesaving tips and easy menu ideas geared to get you in and out of the kitchen—FAST.

The Ultimate Recipe Ingredient
Get a head start in the kitchen and begin with Campbell's condensed soup . . . that's the real secret to making delicious dishes in minutes. Campbell's condensed soups make cooking easy and versatile for new and experienced cooks alike because the rich, delicious flavor eliminates the need for a lot of extra ingredients.

Many of these recipes use budget-easing ingredients for everyday tasty and nourishing meals. Every recipe has been carefully developed and tested by home economists in the Campbell's Creative Food Center ensuring perfect results every time you cook.

Campbell Soup's top-quality standards are reflected in every soup variety and are the beginnings of fabulous meals. There's a wide variety of convenient-to-use cooking soups, choose from cream of mushroom, cream of celery, cream of chicken, cream of broccoli and nacho cheese just to name a few. For a complete line-up, look at the photo of Campbell's Family of Cooking Soups on page 7.

In this fabulous new cookbook, you'll find regional recipe favorites such as spicy Southwestern-style Nacho Chicken Tostadas, Shortcut Brunswick Stew from the South and even a cheesesteak-flavored soup from Philadelphia. For the more adventuresome cook, there's Salsa Swordfish, herbed Vegetable Pilaf and nutty Middle Eastern-Style Dip. Look for the classics, such as Campbell's Classic Glorified Chicken, more popular than ever, which can be made with as many as five different soups, depending on your taste or what's on hand in your cupboard. Broccoli Bake which is similar to classic Green Bean Bake is made with our delicious cream of broccoli soup.

As you turn these pages, look for the step-saving tips designed to speed up meal preparation. Check under the recipe titles for serving ideas geared to make meal planning easy. You'll also find handy ingredient substitutes when you want to change a seasoning or make use of in-season vegetables and herbs. For additional information on ingredient substitutes, refer to the Emergency Substitutions chart on page 7.

Timesaving Symbols

To help you choose the recipe designed for the cooking time you have available, we've divided the main-dish recipes according to the time you need to prepare and cook them. For super-fast recipes, go to the chapter titled 20-Minute Express—each recipe can be prepared and cooked in just 20 minutes. And on days when you have a little more time, try the recipes in the 30-Minute Countdown section. If you choose a main dish from Easy-Going Entrées, give yourself about an hour for assembly and cooking . . . set the table, toss a salad or even kick up your feet and relax while your dinner cooks to perfection. The last two chapters feature fast-cooking side dishes and snacks. Throughout the book, look for these timesaving symbols appearing with many of the recipes.

Microwave: An alternative to conventional cooking when time is of the essence. It's a great way to keep you—and the kitchen—cool during hot weather.

6 Ingredients: Recipes featuring 6 ingredients or less.

Extra-Easy: Fifteen minutes or less to get the ingredients ready to microwave, simmer on the range top or pop in the oven.

Step-saving Tips

Here are nine ways to save time both in the kitchen and at the grocery store. Everyday cooking can be hassle-free when you:

- *Organize your kitchen*
  Store utensils where you use them to save time and steps. Don't clutter up the counter with equipment you rarely use.

  Do keep step-saving appliances handy. Your food processor and blender will help save time if you don't have to pull them from storage to use. Don't let dishes pile up. Clean up after each meal to make your kitchen ideal for timesaving cooking.

- **Keep it easy**

  A quick meal is an easy meal. Depending on how much time you have, choose a main dish from one of the first three chapters. Then add a steamed vegetable, a bowl of soup or toss a green salad with a bottled dressing. If you prefer, start with one of our fast side dishes and broil your favorite fish or meat to go with it. End the meal with some fresh fruit or a refreshing sorbet.

- **Make a grocery list**

  Attach a list of basic ingredients to your refrigerator and note when you're running low. Arrange the items on the list in the order you find them in the supermarket. Check the Food Equivalents Chart on page 94 when you're not sure how many lemons you'll need for a cup of juice or how many potatoes are in a pound.

- **Plan by the week**

  Save time by grocery shopping once a week—no extra time lost in lines and unpacking groceries. Stop for perishables only when you need them—you'll be surprised how much time you save.

- **Keep the basics on hand**

  Store the makings of several meals on your shelf and in your refrigerator-freezer: Campbell's soups, packaged rice mixes, bottled salad dressings, frozen vegetables, canned tuna, cheese and assorted condiments to name a few.

- **Buy ingredients conveniently prepared**

  Although it may cost a little more, you can save preparation time if you buy foods the way they'll be used in a recipe. For example, look for shredded cheese, boneless chicken breasts, bread crumbs, chopped nuts and cut-up salad ingredients. When unpacking groceries, store similar items together. Keep special areas on your shelves for Campbell's soups, pasta, canned vegetables, dried legumes, sauce mixes, rice mixes and other favorite staples.

- **Assemble all ingredients**

  Get all the ingredients together before starting to cook. You'll speed up preparation and avoid confusion if you're interrupted.

- **Use spare moments**

  If you're between steps in a recipe, go on to the next step and prepare the ingredients. Or, use the time to steam vegetables or cut up fruit for dessert, for example. Keep up with kitchen cleanup and you won't be left with a mess when dinner is ready.

- **Make extra for later**

  Whenever you cook pasta or rice, cook extra to serve later in a salad or as part of another recipe. Leftover meat is easily turned into another meal—look for the many delicious recipes in this book using cooked chicken, for example.

Campbell's *Cooking in Minutes* cookbook is brimming with recipes and ideas guaranteed to streamline your cooking every day of the week. Enjoy!

EMERGENCY SUBSTITUTIONS

When a recipe calls for:	You may substitute:
1 cup fresh whole milk	1 cup 2%, 1% or skim milk, or ½ cup evaporated milk plus ½ cup water
1 cup half-and-half	1 cup less 2 tablespoons whole milk plus 2 tablespoons melted margarine or butter
1 clove garlic	⅛ teaspoon garlic powder or minced dried garlic
1 small onion	1 teaspoon onion powder or 1 tablespoon minced dried onion, rehydrated
1 teaspoon dry mustard	1 tablespoon prepared mustard
1 tablespoon cornstarch (for thickening)	2 tablespoons all-purpose flour or 2 teaspoons quick-cooking tapioca
1 cup sour cream	1 cup plain yogurt
1 cup sliced zucchini	1 cup sliced summer squash
1 tablespoon chopped fresh herbs	1 teaspoon dried herbs, crushed
½ cup granulated sugar	½ cup packed brown sugar
¼ cup honey	¼ cup light corn syrup

Campbell's Family of Cooking Soups

Chicken-Broccoli Divan

One of Campbell's most requested recipes! To serve eight, the recipe can be doubled as in the photo. Pictured opposite and on front cover.

1 pound fresh broccoli, cut into spears, or 1 package (10 ounces) frozen broccoli spears, cooked and drained

1½ cups cubed cooked chicken or turkey

1 can (10¾ ounces) Campbell's condensed cream of broccoli or cream of chicken soup

⅓ cup milk

½ cup shredded Cheddar cheese (2 ounces)

2 tablespoons fine dry bread crumbs

1 tablespoon margarine or butter, melted

1. Preheat oven to 450°F.

2. In 10- by 6-inch baking dish, arrange broccoli; top with chicken. In small bowl, combine soup and milk; pour over chicken. Sprinkle with cheese. In cup, combine bread crumbs and margarine; sprinkle over cheese.

3. Bake 15 minutes or until hot and bubbling. Makes 4 servings.

To microwave: Do not cook broccoli. In 10- by 6-inch microwave-safe baking dish, arrange broccoli. Cover with vented plastic wrap; microwave on HIGH 6 minutes, rearranging broccoli halfway through cooking. Drain. Top with chicken. In small bowl, combine soup and milk; pour over chicken. Sprinkle with cheese. In cup, combine bread crumbs and margarine; sprinkle over cheese. Cover with waxed paper; microwave on HIGH 6 minutes or until heated through, rotating dish halfway through heating.

Chicken-Broccoli Divan

Nacho Chicken Tostadas

To serve as shown in the photo, follow directions below for making Tortilla Cups. Pictured opposite.

1 can (11 ounces) Campbell's condensed nacho cheese soup
2½ cups cubed cooked chicken
1 can (8 ounces) stewed tomatoes
1 can (4 ounces) chopped green chilies, drained

10 purchased tostada shells
5 cups shredded lettuce
Chopped sweet red and yellow peppers for garnish
Fresh cilantro or parsley for garnish

1. In 2-quart saucepan over medium heat, combine soup, chicken, tomatoes and chilies; heat through.

2. On each tostada shell, arrange ½ *cup* of the lettuce. Top with ¼ *cup* of the soup mixture. Garnish with red peppers and cilantro. Makes 10 tostadas or 5 servings.

Tortilla Cups: Preheat oven to 400°F. Use 10 (8-inch) corn tortillas instead of tostada shells. On baking sheet, place 5 balls of aluminum foil (about 4-inch diameter). Spray 10-inch nonstick skillet with vegetable cooking spray. Over high heat, heat *one* corn tortilla 5 seconds on each side until tortilla is softened. Drain on paper towels. Immediately drape tortilla over foil ball on baking sheet. Repeat with 4 additional tortillas. Bake 5 minutes or until golden. Remove from oven and cool on foil balls. Turn tortilla cups over; remove foil balls. Repeat with remaining tortillas. Proceed as directed in step 2. Makes 10 Tortilla Cups.

Easy Basil Chicken with Rice

1 can (10½ ounces) Campbell's condensed chicken broth
1 can (16 ounces) stewed tomatoes
2 cloves garlic, minced
1 teaspoon dried basil leaves, crushed

2 cups cubed cooked chicken
1½ cups quick-cooking rice, uncooked
1 cup frozen peas
¼ teaspoon hot pepper sauce

In 3-quart saucepan over high heat, heat broth, tomatoes, garlic and basil to boiling. Add chicken, rice, peas and hot pepper sauce. Return to boiling. Remove from heat. Cover; let stand 5 minutes or until most of the liquid is absorbed. Fluff rice with fork before serving. Makes 5 cups or 4 servings.

Nacho Chicken Tostadas

Spicy Broccoli Beef

If you use fine egg noodles, they'll cook in less time.

1 can (10½ ounces) Campbell's
    condensed beef broth
½ cup water
2 tablespoons cornstarch
1 tablespoon soy sauce
½ teaspoon crushed red pepper
2 tablespoons peanut oil,
    divided

4 cups broccoli flowerets
2 green onions, diagonally
    sliced
1 pound boneless beef sirloin
    steak, thinly sliced
Hot cooked noodles

1. In bowl, combine broth, water, cornstarch, soy sauce and red pepper; set aside.

2. In 10-inch skillet over high heat, in *1 tablespoon* hot oil, stir-fry broccoli and green onions 2 minutes or until tender-crisp. Transfer to bowl.

3. In same skillet over high heat, in remaining hot oil, stir-fry beef *half* at a time, until color just changes. Transfer to bowl with broccoli.

4. Stir broth mixture into skillet. Cook over high heat until mixture boils and thickens, stirring often. Add broccoli-beef mixture; heat through. Serve over noodles. Serve with additional *soy sauce*, if desired. Makes 4 cups or 4 servings.

Skillet Black-Eyed Peas 'n' Rice

For more zip, increase the amount of hot pepper sauce.

1 package (10 ounces) frozen
    chopped spinach
¾ pound bulk pork sausage
1 medium onion, sliced
2 cloves garlic, minced
1 can (10½ ounces) Campbell's
    condensed beef broth

½ cup water
1 can (16 ounces) black-eyed
    peas, drained
1½ cups quick-cooking rice,
    uncooked
¼ teaspoon hot pepper sauce

1. Cook spinach according to package directions; drain well.

2. Meanwhile, in 10-inch skillet over medium heat, cook sausage, onion and garlic until browned, stirring to separate meat. Spoon off fat. Stir in broth, water and peas. Heat to boiling.

3. Stir in rice, cooked spinach and hot pepper sauce. Heat to boiling. Remove from heat. Cover; let stand 5 minutes or until most of the liquid is absorbed. Fluff rice with fork before serving. Makes 6½ cups or 4 servings.

Szechuan Shredded Pork

Stir chopped fresh parsley, coriander or chives into the rice for added color and flavor.

1½ pounds pork shoulder
    blade steak
1 can (10¾ ounces) Campbell's
    condensed golden
    mushroom soup
½ cup water
¼ cup dry sherry
1 tablespoon soy sauce

½ teaspoon ground ginger
½ teaspoon crushed red pepper
2 tablespoons vegetable oil,
    divided
½ cup diagonally sliced carrot
½ medium sweet red or green
    pepper, cut into 2-inch
    julienne strips
Hot cooked rice

1. Remove bone from steak; thinly slice steak, discarding excess fat. Set aside.

2. In small bowl, combine soup, water, sherry, soy sauce, ginger and crushed red pepper.

3. In 10-inch skillet over high heat, in *1 tablespoon* hot oil, stir-fry carrot and red pepper strips until tender-crisp. Transfer to bowl.

4. In same skillet, in remaining oil, stir-fry pork *half* at a time, until pork is no longer pink. Stir in cooked vegetables and soup mixture. Heat to boiling. Serve over rice. Makes 4 servings.

Speedy Spicy Chili

Pass bowls of chopped tomato, shredded cheese, sliced green onions and sour cream to add pizzazz to this extra-fast chili.

1 pound ground beef
½ cup chopped onion
1 clove garlic, minced
1 tablespoon chili powder
1 can (16 ounces) pork and
    beans in tomato sauce

1 can (10¾ ounces) Campbell's
    condensed tomato soup
1 can (4 ounces) chopped
    green chilies
½ cup water

1. In 10-inch skillet over medium-high heat, cook beef, onion, garlic and chili powder until beef is browned and onion is tender, stirring to separate meat. Spoon off fat.

2. Stir in beans, soup, chilies and water. Heat to boiling. Reduce heat to low. Simmer 10 minutes, stirring occasionally. Makes 4 cups or 4 servings.

Cod Steaks Oriental

Use fresh spinach leaves instead of bok choy if you prefer—just shred coarsely with a sharp knife. Pictured opposite.

½ pound bok choy
2 tablespoons cornstarch
2 tablespoons teriyaki sauce
2 tablespoons dry sherry
1 can (10½ ounces) Campbell's condensed chicken broth
4 green onions, cut into 2-inch diagonal pieces

1 cup sweet red pepper cut into 1-inch strips
⅛ teaspoon crushed red pepper
4 cod or halibut steaks, cut ¾ inch thick (about 2 pounds)

1. Cut bok choy stems into ¼-inch slices; coarsely shred leaves. In cup, stir together cornstarch, teriyaki sauce and sherry until well blended. Set aside.

2. In 10-inch skillet over high heat, combine broth, green onions, red pepper strips, crushed red pepper and bok choy stems. Heat to boiling. Arrange fish over vegetable mixture. Reduce heat to low. Cover; cook 8 to 12 minutes or until fish flakes easily when tested.

3. Transfer fish to platter; keep warm. Stir cornstarch mixture and bok choy leaves into skillet. Cook over high heat until mixture boils and thickens, stirring often. Spoon over fish. Makes 4 servings.

Fettuccine with Mushroom-Clam Sauce

Look for fresh or refrigerated pasta at your supermarket—most cook in 5 minutes or less. You'll need about 8 ounces for 4 servings.

2 cans (6½ ounces *each*) chopped clams
1 tablespoon margarine or butter
2 cloves garlic, minced
¼ cup Chablis or other dry white wine

1 can (10¾ ounces) Campbell's condensed cream of mushroom soup
¼ cup grated Parmesan cheese
Hot cooked fettuccine
Chopped fresh parsley for garnish

1. Drain clams, reserving liquid. In 2-quart saucepan over medium heat, in hot margarine, cook garlic until golden, stirring often.

2. Add clam liquid and wine. Increase heat to high. Boil 6 minutes or until liquid is reduced to ½ cup.

3. Stir in soup, clams and Parmesan. Reduce heat to low. Simmer 3 minutes or until heated through, stirring occasionally. Serve over fettuccine. Garnish with parsley. Makes 4 servings.

Cod Steaks Oriental

Saucy Cheese Tortellini

1 pound fresh or frozen cheese
   tortellini
1 can (10¾ ounces) Campbell's
   condensed cream of
   mushroom soup
1 soup can milk
¾ cup frozen peas
½ cup shredded carrot

⅛ teaspoon freshly ground
   pepper
3 tablespoons grated Parmesan
   cheese
¼ cup chopped fresh parsley
   Chopped toasted walnuts for
   garnish

1. Cook tortellini according to package directions; drain.

2. Meanwhile, in 3-quart saucepan, combine soup, milk, peas, carrot and pepper. Over medium heat, heat to boiling. Reduce heat to low. Cover; simmer 4 minutes or until peas are tender, stirring occasionally.

3. Stir in Parmesan and parsley. Heat until cheese melts. Stir in cooked tortellini. Garnish with walnuts. Makes 5 cups or 4 servings.

> ***Walnuts are easy to toast*** *in your microwave oven. Arrange on a paper towel; microwave on HIGH 45 seconds or until lightly browned.*

Classic Campbelled Eggs

Make with cream of celery, Cheddar cheese, cream of mushroom or nacho cheese soup for a change of pace.

1 can (10¾ ounces) Campbell's
   condensed cream of
   chicken soup
8 eggs, beaten
   Dash pepper

2 tablespoons margarine
   or butter
   Chopped fresh parsley or
   chives for garnish

1. In medium bowl, stir soup until smooth. Gradually blend in eggs and pepper.

2. In 10-inch skillet over low heat, melt margarine. Pour in egg mixture. As eggs begin to set, stir lightly so uncooked egg flows to bottom. Cook until set but still very moist. Garnish with parsley. Serve immediately. Makes 4 servings.

To microwave: Omit margarine. In 3-quart microwave-safe casserole, stir soup until smooth. Gradually blend in eggs and pepper. Cover with lid; microwave on HIGH 6½ minutes or until eggs are nearly set, stirring 3 times during cooking. Let stand, covered, 2 minutes. Garnish with parsley.

Hamburger 'n' Fixings Sandwiches

*Serve an assortment of toppers with this sandwich: chopped onion,
leaf lettuce, pickle relish and sliced tomatoes.*

1 pound ground beef
4 hard rolls (*each* 8 inches
   long), split lengthwise
1 can (10½ ounces) Campbell's
   condensed French
   onion soup

¼ cup ketchup
2 tablespoons finely chopped
   sweet pickle
2 teaspoons spicy brown
   mustard
⅛ teaspoon pepper

1. In 10-inch skillet over medium heat, cook beef until browned,
   stirring to separate meat. Spoon off fat. Meanwhile, toast hard rolls.

2. Stir soup, ketchup, pickle, mustard and pepper into skillet. Heat to
   boiling. Reduce heat to low; heat through. Spoon about ½ *cup* of
   the beef mixture onto each roll bottom. Top with desired toppings.
   Cover with roll tops. Makes 4 servings.

To microwave: In 2-quart microwave-safe casserole, crumble beef.
Cover with lid; microwave on HIGH 5 minutes or until beef is no
longer pink, stirring once during cooking to separate meat. Spoon off
fat. Meanwhile, toast rolls. Stir soup, ketchup, pickle, mustard and
pepper into casserole. Microwave, uncovered, on HIGH 3 to 4 minutes
or until hot and bubbling, stirring 3 times during cooking. Serve as
directed in step 2.

Reuben-Style Skillet

*This flavorful skillet dish will remind you of a classic Reuben
sandwich, minus the sauerkraut. Use coleslaw mix to
save valuable chopping time.*

1 can (10¾ ounces) Campbell's
   condensed cream of
   potato soup
2 tablespoons Thousand Island
   salad dressing
½ cup water
3 cups purchased fresh coleslaw
   mix

2 cups cooked corned beef cut
   into 2-inch julienne strips
2 cups plain croutons
1 cup shredded Swiss cheese
   (4 ounces)
2 tablespoons chopped fresh
   parsley

1. In 10-inch skillet, combine soup, dressing and water. Over high heat,
   heat to boiling. Stir in coleslaw mix. Reduce heat to low. Cover;
   simmer 5 minutes or until cabbage is tender-crisp, stirring twice.

2. Stir in beef. Cover; cook 2 minutes or until heated, stirring once.

3. Combine croutons, cheese and parsley. Sprinkle over mixture;
   heat 2 minutes or until cheese melts. Makes 4 servings.

Easy Turkey Salad

For a no-fuss, keep-cool meal, add a cluster of red grapes and sesame crackers. Pictured opposite.

1 can (10¾ ounces) Campbell's condensed cream of celery soup
½ cup mayonnaise
4 cups chopped cooked turkey
1 cup finely chopped celery
½ cup chopped sweet red pepper
½ cup sliced green onions
2 tablespoons chopped fresh parsley
⅛ teaspoon pepper
Leaf lettuce

In large bowl, stir together soup and mayonnaise until smooth. Fold in turkey, celery, red pepper, onions, parsley and pepper. Serve mixture on leaf lettuce. Cover and refrigerate any remaining salad mixture. Makes about 5 cups or 8 servings.

Pepperoni Pizza Soup

This spicy pizza soup uses the family-sized 26-ounce can of condensed tomato soup. For 2 servings, follow directions below using a 10¾-ounce can of tomato soup.

1 can (26 ounces) Campbell's condensed tomato soup
1 soup can water
⅔ cup sliced pepperoni
1 teaspoon dried Italian seasoning, crushed
Shredded mozzarella cheese
Croutons

In 2-quart saucepan, combine soup, water, pepperoni and Italian seasoning. Over medium heat, heat through. Serve topped with cheese and croutons. Makes 6 cups or 4 servings.

Variation: Substitute ½ pound cooked, drained ground beef for pepperoni.

Pepperoni Pizza Soup for Two: In 1-quart saucepan, combine 1 can (10¾ ounces) Campbell's condensed tomato soup, 1 soup can water, ⅓ cup sliced pepperoni and ½ teaspoon dried Italian seasoning, crushed. Proceed as directed above. Makes 2½ cups or 2 servings.

Easy Turkey Salad

Tuna-Tortellini Soup

Next time use canned, cooked chunk chicken. Pictured opposite.

1 can (10¾ ounces) Campbell's
  condensed cream of
  broccoli soup
1 can (10½ ounces) Campbell's
  condensed chicken broth
1 cup water
¼ teaspoon dried basil leaves,
  crushed
⅛ teaspoon garlic powder

2 cups fresh or frozen cheese
  tortellini
1 cup frozen whole kernel corn
1 cup milk
1 can (6½ ounces) tuna,
  drained
2 tablespoons diced pimento
Chopped fresh parsley
  for garnish

1. In 3-quart saucepan, combine soup, broth, water, basil and garlic. Cover; over high heat, heat to boiling.

2. Add tortellini and corn. Reduce heat to low. Cover; simmer 10 minutes or until tortellini is tender.

3. Stir in milk, tuna and pimento; heat through. Garnish with parsley. Makes 6 cups or 4 servings.

Creamy Shrimp Bisque

2 tablespoons margarine
  or butter
1 cup sliced fresh mushrooms
2 tablespoons sliced green onion
1 clove garlic, minced
1 can (10½ ounces) Campbell's
  condensed chicken broth

1 pound frozen shelled and
  deveined medium shrimp
3 tablespoons all-purpose flour
½ cup light cream
⅓ cup Chablis or other dry
  white wine
1 tablespoon chopped fresh
  parsley

1. In 10-inch skillet over medium heat, in hot margarine, cook mushrooms, green onion and garlic until tender, stirring occasionally. Add broth and shrimp. Heat to boiling.

2. Meanwhile, in cup, stir together flour and cream until well blended. Stir into broth mixture. Cook until mixture boils and thickens, stirring often.

3. Add wine and parsley; heat through. Makes 4 cups or 4 servings.

Tuna-Tortellini Soup

Spicy Bean Soup

Serve this hearty vegetable soup with tortilla chips,
warm flour tortillas or purchased corn muffins.
Pictured opposite.

1 tablespoon vegetable oil
½ cup chopped green pepper
½ cup chopped onion
1 can (10¾ ounces) Campbell's
    condensed tomato soup
1 can (19 ounces) chick peas
    (garbanzo beans), drained

1 can (16 ounces) black beans,
    drained
1 soup can water
1 teaspoon Worcestershire sauce
⅛ teaspoon hot pepper sauce
1 cup shredded Cheddar or
    Monterey Jack cheese
    (4 ounces)

1. In 3-quart saucepan over medium heat, in hot oil, cook green pepper and onion 5 minutes, stirring occasionally.

2. Stir in soup, chick peas, beans, water, Worcestershire and hot pepper sauce. Heat to boiling. Reduce heat to low. Cover; simmer 5 minutes, stirring occasionally. Serve topped with cheese. Makes 6 cups or 4 servings.

> **For a warm bread super-fast,** wrap flour tortillas in plain white paper towels. Microwave on HIGH 30 seconds.

Knockwurst Potato Chowder

2 tablespoons margarine
    or butter
3 knockwurst, cut into ¼-inch
    slices (about 9 ounces)
½ cup finely chopped celery
1 medium onion, finely
    chopped

2 cans (10¾ ounces *each*)
    Campbell's condensed
    cream of potato soup
1 soup can milk
1 cup water
½ cup frozen whole kernel corn
2 tablespoons chopped
    fresh parsley

1. In 4-quart saucepan over high heat, in hot margarine, cook knockwurst, celery and onion until sausage is browned, stirring occasionally. Spoon off fat.

2. Stir in soup, milk, water and corn. Heat to boiling. Reduce heat to low. Cover; simmer 4 minutes or until corn is tender. Stir in parsley. Makes 6¾ cups or 4 servings.

Spicy Bean Soup

Smoked Turkey Bean Soup

Next time use leftover roast turkey or baked ham instead of the smoked turkey breast.

1 tablespoon vegetable oil
1 medium onion, chopped
2 cloves garlic, minced
1 can (10¾ ounces) Campbell's condensed cream of potato soup
1 can (16 ounces) white cannellini beans, drained

1 soup can water
¼ pound smoked turkey breast, cut into ½-inch pieces (about 1 cup)
1 teaspoon paprika
1 tablespoon chopped fresh parsley

1. In 2-quart saucepan over medium heat, in hot oil, cook onion and garlic until tender, stirring occasionally.

2. Stir in soup, beans, water, turkey and paprika. Heat to boiling. Reduce heat to low. Simmer 5 minutes. Stir in parsley. Makes 4½ cups or 3 servings.

Chicken 'n' Shrimp Gumbo

If you're short on time, use two cans (5 ounces each) cooked chunk chicken.

1 can (8 ounces) tomatoes, undrained, cut up
1 tablespoon margarine or butter
½ cup sliced green onions
2 cloves garlic, minced
2 cans (10¾ ounces *each*) Campbell's condensed chicken gumbo soup

1 can (10¾ ounces) Campbell's condensed cream of chicken soup
1 cup chopped cooked chicken
1 teaspoon hot pepper sauce
1 pound frozen shelled and deveined medium shrimp
3 cups hot cooked rice

1. Drain tomatoes, reserving liquid. Add enough water to make *1 cup*; set aside.

2. Meanwhile, in 4-quart saucepan over medium heat, in hot margarine, cook green onions and garlic until onions are tender, stirring occasionally.

3. Add both soups, stirring until smooth. Gradually add tomatoes, reserved liquid, chicken and hot pepper sauce. Cover; heat to boiling.

4. Add shrimp. Reduce heat to low. Cover; cook 8 minutes or until shrimp are pink and opaque, stirring occasionally. Spoon ½ *cup* of the rice into each soup bowl; top with about *1½ cups* of the soup. Makes 8 cups or 5 servings.

Country Ham 'n' Potato Soup

For a change of pace, try other vegetables instead of cabbage, such as: chopped bok choy, romaine or spinach.

1 tablespoon margarine
  or butter
1 cup shredded cabbage
¼ pound fully cooked ham,
  cut into strips
  (1 cup)

1 can (10¾ ounces) Campbell's
  condensed cream of
  potato soup
1 soup can water
1 tablespoon chopped fresh
  parsley

1. In 2-quart saucepan over medium-high heat, in hot margarine, cook cabbage and ham 5 minutes or until cabbage is tender, stirring occasionally.

2. Stir in remaining ingredients. Heat to boiling. Reduce heat to low; heat through. Makes 3½ cups or 2 servings.

Philadelphia Cheesesteak Soup

Here's a spin-off of the popular Philadelphia cheesesteak sandwich. If you like, stir in some sliced hot Italian peppers—that's how many Philadelphians enjoy their cheesesteaks.

2 frozen chipped beef sandwich
  steaks (2 ounces *each*)
2 tablespoons margarine
  or butter
1 medium onion, cut into
  thin wedges
½ small green pepper,
  cut into strips

1 can (11 ounces) Campbell's
  condensed Cheddar cheese
  soup
1 cup water
1 teaspoon Worcestershire
  sauce
1½ cups toasted bread cubes
  (about 1 inch)

1. Cut each steak into 2- by ½-inch strips.

2. In 3-quart saucepan over medium heat, in hot margarine, cook onion and green pepper until tender, stirring occasionally. Add steak strips; cook meat until color just changes, stirring often.

3. Stir in soup until smooth. Gradually stir in water and Worcestershire; heat through. Serve topped with toasted bread cubes. Makes 3 cups or 2 servings.

> ***Toast bread cubes*** *under the broiler. Or use purchased seasoned croutons.*

F lash-in-the-pan skillet meals, fast-fixin' main dishes and snappy stir-fries ready to eat in 30 minutes or less—

Salsa Swordfish

Serve steamed fresh asparagus spears for a quick and colorful accompaniment. Pictured opposite.

1 can (10¾ ounces) Campbell's
    condensed tomato soup
½ cup salsa
2 teaspoons chopped fresh
    cilantro or 1 tablespoon
    chopped fresh parsley

2 teaspoons lemon juice
4 swordfish steaks,
    cut ¾ to 1 inch thick
    (about 2 pounds)
Fresh cilantro or parsley
    for garnish

1. In 10-inch skillet, combine soup, salsa, cilantro and lemon juice. Over high heat, heat to boiling. Arrange steaks in soup mixture. Return to boiling. Reduce heat to low. Cover; simmer 15 minutes or until fish flakes easily when tested with fork.

2. Transfer fish to platter; keep warm. Over medium heat, cook sauce until slightly thickened, stirring occasionally. Serve sauce over fish. Garnish with cilantro. Makes 4 servings.

Dijon Cod Fillets

1 pound cod fillets, cut ½ to
    ¾ inch thick
2 tablespoons margarine
    or butter
1 cup diagonally sliced carrot
1 small onion, finely chopped

¼ cup water
1 can (10¾ ounces) Campbell's
    condensed cream of celery
    soup
2 teaspoons Dijon-style
    mustard
⅛ teaspoon pepper

1. Preheat oven to 400°F. Arrange fish in 12- by 8-inch baking dish. Bake 10 minutes.

2. Meanwhile, in 2-quart saucepan over medium heat, in hot margarine, cook carrot and onion 3 minutes, stirring occasionally. Add water. Cover; cook 5 minutes or until carrot is tender.

3. In bowl, combine soup, mustard and pepper. Spoon over fish. Bake 10 minutes more or until fish flakes easily when tested with fork. Transfer fish to platter. Add cooked carrot and onion to sauce; stir. Spoon over fish. Makes 4 servings.

Salsa Swordfish

Creamy Dill Salmon Steaks

*Purchase a seasoned wild rice combo to serve with this fish—
many cook in just 10 minutes.*

1 tablespoon margarine or butter	2 tablespoons Chablis or other dry white wine
½ cup chopped green onions	2 tablespoons chopped fresh dill or 1 teaspoon dried dill weed, crushed
1 can (10¾ ounces) Campbell's condensed cream of celery soup	4 salmon steaks, cut 1 inch thick (about 2 pounds)
½ cup half-and-half	

1. In 10-inch skillet over medium heat, in hot margarine, cook green onions until tender, stirring often. Add soup, half-and-half, wine and dill; stir until smooth.

2. Arrange fish steaks in soup mixture. Heat to boiling. Reduce heat to low. Cover; simmer 15 minutes or until fish flakes easily when tested with fork. Makes 4 servings.

To microwave: In 12- by 8-inch microwave-safe baking dish, combine margarine and green onions. Cover with vented plastic wrap; microwave on HIGH 2 minutes or until onions are tender, stirring once during cooking. Add soup, half-and-half, wine and dill; stir until smooth. Arrange fish steaks in dish with thicker portions of fish toward outside of dish. Cover; microwave on HIGH 10 to 11 minutes or until fish flakes easily when tested with fork, rotating dish twice during cooking. Let stand, covered, 5 minutes before serving.

Fish with Swiss Cheese Sauce

*Drizzle sliced cucumbers and onions with a tangy vinaigrette for an
easy, great-tasting salad that complements this fish dish.*

6 flounder fillets, cut about ¼ inch thick (about 1½ pounds)	2 tablespoons Chablis or other dry white wine
1 can (10¾ ounces) Campbell's condensed cream of mushroom soup	½ cup shredded Swiss cheese (2 ounces)
	1 tablespoon chopped fresh parsley

1. Preheat oven to 400°F. In 13- by 9-inch baking dish, arrange fish fillets in a single layer. Bake 10 minutes.

2. Meanwhile, in small bowl, combine soup and wine. Pour soup mixture over fillets, stirring into cooking liquid. Sprinkle with cheese and parsley. Bake 5 minutes more or until fish flakes easily when tested with fork. Makes 6 servings.

Cheesy Tuna and Twists

*For a heartier cheese flavor, use sharp Cheddar
instead of mozzarella.*

8 ounces corkscrew macaroni,
  uncooked
2 tablespoons margarine
  or butter
1 package (10 ounces) frozen
  mixed vegetables, thawed
1 clove garlic, minced
1 can (10¾ ounces) Campbell's
  condensed cream of
  mushroom soup

¾ cup milk
1½ cups shredded mozzarella
  cheese (6 ounces)
⅛ teaspoon pepper
  Generous dash ground
  nutmeg
1 can (6½ ounces) tuna,
  drained
  Chopped pimento for garnish

1. Cook macaroni according to package directions; drain.

2. Meanwhile, in 10-inch skillet over medium heat, in hot margarine,
   cook mixed vegetables and garlic 2 minutes, stirring often.

3. Add soup to skillet; stir until smooth. Gradually stir in milk. Add
   cheese, pepper and nutmeg; heat until cheese melts, stirring
   occasionally.

4. Stir in tuna and cooked macaroni. Heat through. Garnish with
   pimento. Makes 6 cups or 4 servings.

Broccoli Fish Chowder

Use haddock, halibut or cod in this vegetable chowder.

3 tablespoons margarine
  or butter
1 cup sliced celery
1 cup chopped onions
2 cloves garlic, minced
¼ cup Chablis or other dry
  white wine
2 cans (10¾ ounces *each*)
  Campbell's condensed
  cream of broccoli soup

2 cups milk
1 pound firm white fish fillets,
  cut into 1-inch pieces
2 tablespoons diced pimento
  Generous dash ground
  red pepper

1. In 3-quart saucepan over medium heat, in hot margarine, cook
   celery, onions and garlic until tender, stirring often.

2. Add wine; cook 2 minutes. Add soup; stir until smooth. Gradually
   stir in milk. Add fish, pimento and red pepper. Heat to boiling.
   Reduce heat to low. Cover; simmer 5 minutes or until fish flakes
   easily when tested with fork. Makes 3½ cups or 4 servings.

Curried Chicken-Vegetable Chowder

Serve with classic oyster crackers or pass a basket of seasoned pita chips or bagel chips. Pictured opposite.

1 can (10¾ ounces) Campbell's condensed cream of chicken soup
1 can (10½ ounces) Campbell's condensed chicken broth
2 cups water
½ teaspoon curry powder
⅛ teaspoon dried thyme leaves, crushed
⅛ teaspoon pepper
2 cups cubed peeled potatoes (3 medium)
2 cups cubed cooked chicken
1 cup broccoli flowerets
1 cup sliced fresh mushrooms
½ cup sweet red pepper cut in strips

1. In 3-quart saucepan, stir soup until smooth. Gradually stir in broth, water, curry, thyme and pepper. Over medium heat, heat to boiling. Add potatoes. Boil 10 minutes.

2. Add remaining ingredients. Reduce heat to low. Cover; simmer 5 minutes or until vegetables are tender. Makes 8 cups or 6 servings.

Lemon-Broccoli Chicken
6 OR LESS

This easy skillet dish is one of Campbell's most popular recipes according to a recent consumer survey.

1 lemon
1 tablespoon vegetable oil
2 whole chicken breasts, split, skinned and boned (about 1 pound boneless)
1 can (10¾ ounces) Campbell's condensed cream of broccoli or cream of mushroom soup
¼ cup milk
⅛ teaspoon pepper

1. Cut 4 thin slices of lemon; set aside. Squeeze 2 teaspoons juice from remaining lemon; set aside.

2. In 10-inch skillet over medium heat, in hot oil, cook chicken 10 minutes or until browned on both sides. Spoon off fat.

3. Meanwhile, in small bowl, combine soup and milk; stir in reserved lemon juice and pepper. Pour over chicken; top each chicken piece with lemon slice.

4. Reduce heat to low. Cover; simmer 5 minutes or until chicken is tender and juices run clear, stirring occasionally. Makes 4 servings.

Curried Chicken-Vegetable Chowder

Chicken with Julienne Vegetables

Look for packaged spinach noodle nests at your supermarket. Or make your own by twirling cooked pasta with fork before serving. Pictured opposite.

1 can (10¾ ounces) Campbell's condensed creamy chicken mushroom soup
¼ cup milk
¼ teaspoon dried thyme leaves, crushed
2 whole chicken breasts, split, skinned and boned (about 1 pound boneless)

2 cups carrots cut in 2-inch julienne strips
2 cups zucchini cut in 2-inch julienne strips
Fresh thyme leaves for garnish

1. In 10-inch skillet, combine soup, milk and dried thyme. Over medium heat, heat to boiling. Add chicken and carrots. Reduce heat to low. Cover; simmer 10 minutes, stirring occasionally.

2. Add zucchini. Cover; cook 5 minutes or until chicken is tender and juices run clear. Garnish with fresh thyme. Makes 4 servings.

Broccoli Chicken Dijon

Fresh broccoli flowerets can be used instead of frozen— just steam until tender-crisp.

2 cups frozen cut broccoli (8 ounces)
2 tablespoons vegetable oil
1 pound boneless chicken breasts, cut into 2- by 1-inch strips
1 can (10¾ ounces) Campbell's condensed cream of broccoli soup

½ soup can milk
½ cup shredded Swiss cheese (2 ounces)
2 tablespoons Dijon-style mustard
2 tablespoons chopped pimento
Hot cooked rice

1. Prepare broccoli according to package directions; drain.

2. Meanwhile, in 10-inch skillet over medium-high heat, in hot oil, stir-fry chicken until browned.

3. Stir in soup, milk, cheese, mustard, pimento and cooked broccoli. Heat to boiling. Reduce heat to low. Cover; simmer 5 minutes, stirring occasionally. Serve over rice. Makes 4 cups or 4 servings.

Chicken with Julienne Vegetables

Chicken Pineapple Stir-Fry

Save time by cutting up vegetables and chicken in advance.

1 can (8 ounces) pineapple
    chunks
1 can (10½ ounces) Campbell's
    condensed chicken broth
2 tablespoons cornstarch
2 tablespoons soy sauce
¼ teaspoon ground ginger

2 tablespoons vegetable oil
2 cups broccoli flowerets
½ cup diagonally sliced carrot
2 cups cubed cooked chicken
    or turkey
Hot cooked rice

1. Drain pineapple, reserving juice. In small bowl, combine reserved juice, broth, cornstarch, soy sauce and ginger; set aside.

2. In 10-inch skillet over high heat, in hot oil, stir-fry broccoli and carrot until tender-crisp.

3. Stir in chicken and broth mixture. Reduce heat to medium-high. Cook until mixture boils and thickens, stirring often. Add pineapple; heat through. Serve over rice. Serve with additional *soy sauce*, if desired. Makes 4½ cups or 4 servings.

If you cook one pound boneless chicken breasts in advance, you'll be able to prepare any dish that calls for cubed cooked chicken. Each pound of chicken yields 2 cups cubed chicken.

Chicken in Spicy Peanut Sauce

3 whole chicken breasts, split,
    skinned and boned (about
    1½ pounds boneless)
2 tablespoons vegetable oil
1 can (10¾ ounces) Campbell's
    condensed cream of
    chicken soup

3 tablespoons chunky peanut
    butter
⅔ cup water
2 green onions, sliced
1 teaspoon chili powder
⅛ teaspoon ground red pepper

1. Place chicken breasts between 2 sheets of plastic wrap. With meat mallet or rolling pin, pound to ¼-inch thickness.

2. In 10-inch skillet over medium heat, in hot oil, cook chicken 10 minutes or until browned on both sides. Remove chicken from skillet. Spoon off fat.

3. Add soup, peanut butter, water, green onions, chili powder and red pepper to skillet; stir until smooth. Over medium heat, heat to boiling. Reduce heat to low. Return chicken to skillet. Cover; simmer 5 minutes or until chicken is tender and juices run clear. Makes 6 servings.

Mandarin Chicken

1 can (10½ ounces) Campbell's
    condensed chicken broth,
    divided
2 tablespoons cornstarch
¼ cup vinegar
¼ cup sugar
1 tablespoon soy sauce
½ teaspoon ground ginger
1 can (8 ounces) sliced water
    chestnuts, drained

1 pound skinless, boneless
    chicken breasts, cut into
    1-inch chunks
1 small green or sweet red
    pepper, cut into strips
1 can (11 ounces) mandarin
    orange segments, drained
Hot cooked rice

1. In cup, stir together ¼ *cup* of the broth and the cornstarch until well blended; set aside.

2. In 10-inch skillet over medium heat, combine remaining broth, vinegar, sugar, soy sauce, ginger and water chestnuts. Heat to boiling.

3. Add chicken to skillet. Reduce heat to low. Simmer 10 minutes. Add green pepper; cook 3 minutes more or until chicken is tender and juices run clear.

4. Stir in cornstarch mixture. Cook over medium heat until mixture boils and thickens, stirring constantly. Gently stir in oranges. Serve over rice. Makes 4 cups or 4 servings.

Souper Chicken Tetrazzini

8 ounces spaghetti, uncooked
2 tablespoons margarine
    or butter
2 cups sliced fresh mushrooms
1 small onion, chopped
2 cans (10¾ ounces) Campbell's
    condensed cream of
    chicken soup

1 soup can milk
2 tablespoons dry sherry
2 cups cubed cooked chicken
⅓ cup grated Parmesan cheese
¼ cup chopped fresh parsley

1. Cook spaghetti according to package directions; drain.

2. Meanwhile, in 2-quart saucepan over medium heat, in hot margarine, cook mushrooms and onion until tender, stirring occasionally. Stir in soup, milk and sherry; heat through.

3. Return cooked spaghetti to cooking pot. Add soup mixture, chicken, Parmesan and parsley. Toss lightly until spaghetti is coated. Over medium heat, heat through. Serve with additional *Parmesan*, if desired. Makes 6 cups or 4 servings.

Garden-Style Vegetable Bisque

Serve with hot garlic bread and a tossed green salad.
Pictured opposite.

2 tablespoons margarine
   or butter
1 small zucchini, halved
   lengthwise and cut into
   ½-inch slices
2 medium carrots, cut into
   2-inch julienne strips
½ cup thinly sliced celery
1 clove garlic, minced
½ teaspoon dried oregano
   leaves, crushed

1 can (11 ounces) Campbell's
   condensed Cheddar cheese
   soup
1 can (10¾ ounces) Campbell's
   condensed cream of
   potato soup
1 soup can milk
1 soup can water
1½ cups chopped cooked chicken
1 medium tomato, seeded and
   chopped

1. In 3-quart saucepan over medium heat, in hot margarine, cook zucchini, carrots, celery, garlic and oregano 10 minutes or until vegetables are tender, stirring occasionally.

2. Add soups, milk and water; stir until smooth. Stir in chicken and tomato. Cover; heat through, stirring occasionally. Makes 7½ cups or 5 servings.

Easy Creole Soup EXTRA EASY

This Southern-style soup uses the family-sized 26-ounce can of condensed tomato soup. For 2 servings, follow the directions below using a 10¾-ounce can of tomato soup.

1 can (26 ounces) Campbell's
   condensed tomato soup
1 soup can water
1 large green pepper, chopped
1 medium onion, chopped

1 cup cooked rice
1 cup coarsely chopped cooked
   shrimp
½ teaspoon Louisiana-style
   hot sauce

In 2½-quart saucepan, combine all ingredients. Over medium heat, heat through. Makes 7⅔ cups or 6 servings.

Creole Soup For Two: In 1½-quart saucepan, combine 1 can (10¾ ounces) Campbell's condensed tomato soup and 1 soup can water. Halve remaining ingredients. Proceed as directed above. Makes 3½ cups or 2 servings.

Garden-Style Vegetable Bisque

Cheeseburger Pizza

This giant open-face cheeseburger tastes good topped with any of your favorite burger fixings. Pictured opposite.

2 packages (7½ ounces *each*) refrigerated biscuits
¾ pound ground beef
½ cup chopped onion
1 can (11 ounces) Campbell's condensed Cheddar cheese soup
1 can (8 ounces) tomatoes, drained, cut up

2 tablespoons sliced green onion
2 teaspoons prepared mustard
⅛ teaspoon hot pepper sauce
½ cup shredded mozzarella cheese (2 ounces)
Sliced onion, hamburger dill pickle chips, mustard and ketchup for garnish

1. Preheat oven to 400°F. Meanwhile, press biscuits into 12-inch round on greased baking sheet or 12-inch pizza pan, pinching edges of biscuits together to seal. Bake 10 minutes.

2. Meanwhile, in 10-inch skillet over medium heat, cook beef and onion until beef is browned and onion is tender, stirring to separate meat. Spoon off fat. Stir in next five ingredients. Heat through.

3. Spread beef mixture over biscuits to within ½ inch of edge. Sprinkle with cheese. Bake 5 minutes or until biscuits are golden brown. Garnish as desired. Cut into wedges. Makes 6 servings.

Meatball Mushroom Sandwiches

½ pound ground beef
½ pound Italian sausage, casing removed
¼ cup fine dry bread crumbs
1 egg, beaten
½ teaspoon dried oregano leaves, crushed
2 tablespoons vegetable oil

1 can (10¾ ounces) Campbell's condensed golden mushroom soup
½ cup water
4 long hard rolls (*each* 8 inches long), split lengthwise

1. In medium bowl, combine beef, sausage, bread crumbs, egg and oregano; mix lightly, but well. Shape into 16 (1½-inch) meatballs.

2. In 10-inch skillet over medium heat, in hot oil, cook meatballs 10 minutes or until browned on all sides. Spoon off fat.

3. Stir in soup and water. Heat to boiling. Reduce heat to low. Cover; simmer 10 minutes or until meatballs are thoroughly cooked, stirring occasionally. Spoon 4 meatballs and about ¼ *cup* of the sauce onto each roll. Makes 4 servings.

Cheeseburger Pizza

Piquant Pork Chops

Accompany with a fresh fruit salad sprinkled with a little lemon or lime juice.

4 boneless pork chops, cut
  ½ inch thick (about
  1 pound)
¼ teaspoon pepper
1 tablespoon vegetable oil
1 can (10½ ounces) Campbell's
  condensed chicken broth

3 tablespoons lime juice
1 tablespoon sugar
1 teaspoon Dijon-style mustard
4 teaspoons cornstarch
2 tablespoons water
  Hot cooked rice

1. Sprinkle pork chops with pepper. In 10-inch skillet over medium heat, in hot oil, cook chops until browned on both sides.

2. Stir in broth, lime juice, sugar and mustard. Heat to boiling. Reduce heat to low. Cover; simmer 10 minutes or until chops are no longer pink.

3. Transfer chops to platter. In cup, stir together cornstarch and water until well blended; gradually stir into skillet. Cook over high heat until mixture boils and thickens, stirring often. Serve with rice. Makes 4 servings.

Garlic Orange Beef

3 tablespoons vegetable oil,
  divided
1 pound boneless beef sirloin
  steak, thinly sliced
1 medium onion, chopped
1 clove garlic, minced
1 teaspoon orange peel cut in
  1-inch-long thin strips
1 can (10¾ ounces) Campbell's
  condensed beefy mushroom
  soup

⅓ cup water
¼ cup tomato paste
¼ cup orange juice
2 tablespoons molasses
⅛ teaspoon pepper
  Hot cooked noodles

1. In 10-inch skillet over high heat, in *2 tablespoons* hot oil, cook *half* the beef until color just changes, stirring often. Transfer beef to bowl. Repeat with remaining beef.

2. Reduce heat to medium. In remaining oil, cook onion, garlic and orange peel 3 minutes, stirring often.

3. Stir in soup, water, tomato paste, orange juice, molasses and pepper. Heat to boiling. Reduce heat to low; simmer 5 minutes. Add beef; cook 5 minutes more, stirring occasionally. Serve over noodles. Makes 3½ cups or 4 servings.

Cincinnati Chili

1 pound ground beef
1 cup chopped green pepper
½ cup chopped onion
2 cloves garlic, minced
3 tablespoons chili powder
2 cans (10¾ ounces) Campbell's
   condensed tomato soup

1 can (15 ounces) kidney beans,
   undrained
1 tablespoon vinegar
¼ teaspoon ground cinnamon
   Hot cooked spaghetti
   Shredded Cheddar cheese
     for garnish
   Sour cream for garnish

1. In 4-quart saucepan over medium heat, cook beef, green pepper, onion, garlic and chili powder until beef is browned and vegetables are tender, stirring to separate meat. Spoon off fat.

2. Stir in soup, kidney beans, vinegar and cinnamon. Heat to boiling. Reduce heat to low. Simmer 15 minutes, stirring occasionally. Serve chili over spaghetti. Garnish with cheese and sour cream. Makes 6 cups or 5 servings.

> *To reheat spaghetti in your microwave oven, place in microwave-safe casserole. Cover with vented plastic wrap; microwave on HIGH 2 minutes for each 1-cup serving. Stir after every 2 minutes of heating.*

Bean-and-Bacon Mac Skillet

3 slices bacon, cut into 1-inch
   pieces
1 small onion, chopped
3½ cups water
2 cups elbow macaroni,
   uncooked
1 can (11 ounces) Campbell's
   condensed Cheddar cheese
   soup

1 can (11 ounces) Campbell's
   condensed nacho cheese
   soup
1 can (16 ounces) kidney beans,
   drained
1 medium tomato, chopped
1 cup shredded Cheddar cheese
   Chopped green onions for
     garnish

1. In 10-inch skillet over medium heat, cook bacon and onion until bacon is crisp, stirring occasionally.

2. Add water. Heat to boiling. Add macaroni. Cook 10 to 12 minutes or until macaroni is tender, stirring often.

3. In large bowl, stir soups until smooth. Add beans, tomato and macaroni mixture; toss lightly to mix. Return to skillet. Cover; cook over low heat 5 minutes or until heated through, stirring occasionally. Sprinkle with cheese. Garnish with green onions. Makes 6 cups or 6 servings.

Pineapple Beef Curry

Be creative with the condiments: chopped green and sweet red peppers, sliced green onions, canned pineapple chunks, flaked coconut, mandarin orange segments and peanuts. Pictured opposite.

1 pound ground beef
2 teaspoons curry powder
1 can (10½ ounces) Campbell's condensed beef broth
1 can (8 ounces) tomatoes, drained, cut up
1 can (8 ounces) crushed pineapple in juice, undrained

3 tablespoons tomato paste
2 tablespoons apricot preserves
4 green onions, diagonally sliced
Hot cooked rice
Assorted condiments (see suggestions above)

1. In 10-inch skillet over medium heat, cook beef until browned, stirring to separate meat. Add curry; cook 2 minutes more.

2. Stir in broth, tomatoes, pineapple, tomato paste and preserves. Heat to boiling. Reduce heat to low. Simmer 10 minutes, stirring occasionally.

3. Stir in green onions; simmer 5 minutes more or until tender, stirring occasionally. Serve over rice with assorted condiments. Makes 4 cups or 4 servings.

Southwest Mac and Beef

For extra fire, serve with hot chili peppers.

1 pound ground beef
1 medium onion, chopped
½ teaspoon ground cumin
1 can (11 ounces) Campbell's condensed Cheddar cheese soup
1 can (10½ ounces) Campbell's condensed beef broth

1 soup can water
1 can (15 ounces) stewed tomatoes
1 can (4 ounces) chopped green chilies
½ cup elbow macaroni, uncooked

1. In 4-quart Dutch oven over medium heat, cook beef, onion and cumin until beef is browned, stirring to separate meat. Spoon off fat.

2. Add soup; stir until smooth. Stir in broth, water, tomatoes and chilies. Heat to boiling. Add macaroni. Reduce heat to low. Cook 12 minutes or until macaroni is tender, stirring occasionally. Makes 6 cups or 4 servings.

Pineapple Beef Curry

Taco Salad

Let everyone build their own salad—just assemble the ingredients in advance. Pictured opposite.

1 pound ground beef
¼ cup chopped onion
1 tablespoon chili powder
1 can (11 ounces) Campbell's condensed nacho cheese soup
1 can (16 ounces) pinto beans, drained

4 cups torn mixed salad greens
Tortilla chips
Chopped fresh tomato
Sliced avocado for garnish
Sliced pitted ripe olives for garnish

1. In 10-inch skillet over medium heat, cook beef, onion and chili powder until beef is browned, stirring to separate meat. Spoon off fat.

2. Stir in soup and beans. Heat to boiling. Reduce heat to low. Simmer 5 minutes, stirring occasionally.

3. Arrange salad greens and tortilla chips on serving plate. Top with hot meat mixture. Top with tomato. Garnish as desired. Serve with additional *tortilla chips*, if desired. Makes 4 servings.

Anise Beef and Rice

2 tablespoons vegetable oil
1 pound boneless top round beef steak, thinly sliced
3 cups coarsely chopped bok choy
½ cup yellow squash cut in 2-inch julienne strips
1 can (10½ ounces) Campbell's condensed beef broth

¼ cup dry sherry
2 tablespoons soy sauce
¼ teaspoon anise seed
2 tablespoons cornstarch
½ cup water
1 cup cherry tomatoes *each* cut in half
Hot cooked rice

1. In 10-inch skillet over high heat, in hot oil, cook beef *half* at a time, until beef just changes color, stirring constantly. Transfer to bowl.

2. Add bok choy and squash to skillet. Over high heat, cook 1 minute, stirring often. Stir in broth, sherry, soy sauce and anise. Heat to boiling.

3. Meanwhile, in cup, stir together cornstarch and water until well blended; gradually stir into broth mixture. Cook until mixture boils and thickens, stirring often. Add cooked beef and cherry tomatoes. Cook 2 minutes or until heated through, stirring often. Serve over rice. Makes 5 cups or 4 servings.

Taco Salad

Cheesy Mushroom Frittata

Serve with fresh fruit or mini croissants. Pictured opposite.

1 can (10¾ ounces) Campbell's condensed cream of mushroom soup
6 eggs, slightly beaten
1½ cups shredded mozzarella cheese (6 ounces), divided
¼ teaspoon dried basil leaves, crushed
⅛ teaspoon pepper

2 tablespoons margarine or butter
1 cup sliced fresh mushrooms
1 medium onion, chopped
Chopped fresh parsley for garnish
Tomato wedges for garnish
Fresh basil leaves for garnish

1. In medium bowl with wire whisk, beat soup until smooth. Gradually blend in eggs, *1 cup* of the cheese, the basil and pepper.

2. In 10-inch *oven-safe* omelet pan or skillet over medium heat, in hot margarine, cook mushrooms and onion until mushrooms are tender and liquid is evaporated, stirring occasionally.

3. Pour mixture into skillet. Reduce heat to low. Cook 6 minutes or until eggs are set 1 inch from edge. *Do not stir*. Remove from heat.

4. Broil 6 inches from heat 5 minutes or until frittata is puffy and lightly browned. Top with remaining cheese. Cover; let stand 2 minutes or until cheese melts. Garnish with parsley, tomato wedges and fresh basil. Makes 5 servings.

Bavarian Kielbasa with Noodles

6 ounces egg noodles, uncooked
¾ pound smoked kielbasa, cut up
1 medium onion, sliced
1 can (10¾ ounces) Campbell's condensed cream of mushroom soup

1 soup can milk
1½ cups frozen cut green beans
⅛ teaspoon pepper
Spicy brown mustard (optional)

1. Cook noodles according to package directions; drain. Meanwhile, in 10-inch skillet over medium heat, cook kielbasa and onion until browned, stirring often. Spoon off fat.

2. Add soup; stir until smooth. Gradually stir in milk. Add beans and pepper. Heat to boiling. Reduce heat to low. Cover; simmer 5 minutes or until beans are tender, stirring occasionally.

3. Stir cooked noodles into skillet. Heat 2 minutes, stirring often. Serve with mustard, if desired. Makes 6 cups or 4 servings.

Cheesy Mushroom Frittata

Fiesta Eggs 〰〰〰 *6 OR LESS*

For a Mexican flair, omit the potatoes and wrap eggs in warmed corn tortillas.

4 frozen shredded potato patties
1 can (11 ounces) Campbell's
    condensed nacho cheese
    soup, divided
8 eggs, slightly beaten
2 tablespoons milk
2 tablespoons margarine
    or butter

1 cup shredded Monterey Jack
    cheese (4 ounces)
Sliced green onions for
    garnish
Chopped sweet red pepper
    for garnish

1. Prepare potato patties according to package directions.

2. Meanwhile, in medium bowl, stir *½ can* of the soup until smooth. Gradually blend in eggs.

3. For sauce: In 1-quart saucepan, combine remaining soup and milk. Over medium heat, heat through, stirring constantly. Cover; keep warm.

4. In 10-inch skillet over medium heat, in hot margarine, cook egg mixture. As eggs begin to set, stir lightly so uncooked egg flows to bottom. Cook until eggs are set but still moist.

5. Sprinkle *¼ cup* of the cheese over each cooked potato patty. Bake until cheese melts.

6. Arrange eggs on top of each potato patty; spoon about *2 tablespoons* of the sauce over each. Garnish with green onions and red pepper. Makes 4 servings.

To microwave: Omit margarine. Prepare potato patties as directed in step 1. Meanwhile, in 3-quart microwave-safe casserole, stir *½ can* of the soup until smooth. Gradually blend in eggs. Cover with lid; microwave on HIGH 6½ minutes or until eggs are nearly set, stirring 3 times during cooking. Let stand, covered, 2 minutes. For sauce: In 1-quart casserole, stir remaining soup until smooth. Stir in milk. Cover with lid; microwave on HIGH 2 minutes or until hot, stirring once during cooking. Serve as directed in step 6.

Sausage Skillet Dinner

To save time, purchase prepared coleslaw at a deli or supermarket to complete this skillet meal.

1 pound smoked kielbasa, cut into ½-inch slices

1 can (10½ ounces) Campbell's condensed French onion soup

¼ cup water

2 cups frozen mixed vegetables

1 can (8 ounces) tomatoes, undrained, cut up

⅛ teaspoon pepper

1½ cups quick-cooking rice, uncooked

Chopped fresh parsley for garnish

1. In 10-inch skillet over medium heat, cook sausage until browned, stirring often. Spoon off fat.

2. Add soup, water, vegetables, tomatoes and pepper. Heat to boiling. Reduce heat to low. Simmer 2 minutes or until vegetables are tender. Stir in rice. Remove from heat. Cover; let stand 5 minutes or until most of the liquid is absorbed. Fluff rice with fork before serving. Garnish with parsley. Makes 6 cups or 4 servings.

Hearty Sausage 'n' Cabbage Soup

Serve with slices of crusty rye or pumpernickel bread.

½ pound ground beef

½ pound Italian sausage, casing removed

2 cups coarsely chopped cabbage

½ cup finely chopped carrot

1 can (10¾ ounces) Campbell's condensed golden mushroom soup

1 can (10½ ounces) Campbell's condensed French onion soup

2 soup cans water

1 can (16 ounces) whole potatoes, drained, cut into 1-inch pieces

1. In 5-quart Dutch oven over high heat, cook beef and sausage until browned, stirring to separate meat.

2. Add cabbage and carrot. Cook 5 minutes, stirring often. Spoon off fat.

3. Stir in soups, water and potatoes. Heat to boiling. Reduce heat to low. Cover; simmer 10 minutes or until carrots are tender. Makes about 7 cups or 5 servings.

Turkey-Vegetable Pot Pie

Toss together a garden salad while this bakes. For a different touch, add sunflower seeds, sliced red onions and snipped dried apricots to the salad greens. Pictured opposite.

1 package (16 ounces) frozen mixed vegetables (broccoli, cauliflower and carrots)

2 tablespoons margarine or butter

½ cup chopped onion

½ cup sliced celery

½ teaspoon dried thyme leaves, crushed

1 can (10¾ ounces) Campbell's condensed cream of broccoli soup

1 can (10¾ ounces) Campbell's condensed cream of chicken soup

1 cup milk

3 cups diced cooked turkey or chicken

¼ teaspoon pepper

1 package (8 ounces) refrigerated crescent rolls

1. Preheat oven to 375°F. Cook vegetables according to package directions; drain.

2. Meanwhile, in 2-quart saucepan over medium heat, in hot margarine, cook onion, celery and thyme until onion is tender, stirring occasionally. Add soups and milk; stir until smooth.

3. In 12- by 8-inch baking dish, combine turkey, cooked vegetables and pepper. Add soup mixture, stirring gently to mix.

4. Unroll crescent rolls without separating pieces. Firmly press perforations to seal. Cut dough lengthwise into 8 strips, about ¾ inch wide. Arrange dough strips over chicken mixture to form a lattice, cutting strips as necessary to fit. Press ends of strips to baking dish.

5. Bake 30 minutes or until golden brown. Cover edges with foil after 20 minutes of baking if pastry browns too quickly. Makes 6 servings.

Turkey-Vegetable Pot Pie

Chicken Enchiladas

Corn tortillas can be substituted for the flour ones.

1 can (10¾ ounces) Campbell's
   condensed cream of celery
   soup
½ cup sour cream
2 tablespoons margarine
   or butter
½ cup chopped onion

1 teaspoon chili powder
2 cups diced cooked chicken
1 can (4 ounces) chopped
   green chilies
8 flour tortillas (7-inch)
1 cup shredded Monterey Jack
   cheese (4 ounces)

1. Preheat oven to 375°F. In small bowl, stir together soup and sour cream until smooth; set aside.

2. In 2-quart saucepan over medium heat, in hot margarine, cook onion and chili powder until onion is tender, stirring often. Stir in chicken, chilies and *2 tablespoons* of the soup mixture. Remove from heat.

3. To make enchiladas: Along center of each tortilla, spread about ¼ *cup* of the chicken mixture; fold sides over filling and place seam-side down in greased 12- by 8-inch baking dish.

4. Spread remaining soup mixture over enchiladas. Cover with foil; bake 15 minutes. Sprinkle with cheese. Bake, uncovered, 5 minutes more or until cheese melts. Makes 4 servings.

Classic Glorified Chicken

A Campbell recipe collection favorite because it's so easy to prepare and uses only three ingredients!

2½- to 3-pound broiler-fryer
   chicken, cut up
1 tablespoon margarine or
   butter, melted

1 can (10¾ ounces) Campbell's
   condensed cream of
   chicken, cream of celery,
   cream of mushroom, golden
   mushroom or cream of
   broccoli soup
Chopped fresh parsley for
   garnish

1. Preheat oven to 375°F. Meanwhile, in 12- by 8-inch baking dish, arrange chicken skin-side up. Drizzle with margarine. Bake 40 minutes.

2. Spoon soup over chicken. Bake 20 minutes more or until chicken is tender and juices run clear. Transfer chicken to platter. Stir sauce; spoon sauce over chicken. Garnish with parsley. Makes 4 servings.

Country-Style Smothered Chicken

2 slices bacon
2½-to 3-pound broiler-fryer
    chicken, cut up
1 can (10¾ ounces) Campbell's
    condensed cream of
    mushroom soup

1 clove garlic, minced
1 teaspoon dried basil leaves,
    crushed
1 medium onion, sliced
    Hot cooked rice

1. In 10-inch skillet over medium heat, cook bacon until crisp. Transfer to paper towels to drain, reserving drippings in pan. Crumble bacon; set aside.

2. Over medium heat, in hot drippings, cook chicken 10 minutes or until browned on all sides. Spoon off fat.

3. Add soup, garlic and basil; stir until smooth. Heat to boiling. Reduce heat to low. Cover; simmer 20 minutes.

4. Add onion. Cover; simmer 15 minutes more or until chicken is tender and juices run clear, stirring occasionally. Sprinkle with crumbled bacon. Serve with rice. Makes 6 servings.

> *For crisp bacon in a hurry, microwave it. One slice of bacon cooks in about one minute.*

Shortcut Brunswick Stew

2 slices bacon
½ cup chopped onion
1 can (10¾ ounces) Campbell's
    condensed tomato soup
1 soup can water
1 teaspoon Worcestershire
    sauce

Generous dash pepper
1 package (10 ounces) frozen
    Fordhook lima beans
1 package (10 ounces) frozen
    whole kernel corn
2 cups cubed cooked chicken

1. In 3-quart saucepan over low heat, cook bacon until crisp. Transfer to paper towels to drain, reserving *1 tablespoon* drippings in pan. Crumble bacon; set aside.

2. Over medium heat, in hot drippings, cook onion until tender, stirring occasionally.

3. Stir in soup, water, Worcestershire and pepper. Heat to boiling. Add lima beans and corn. Return to boiling. Stir to separate vegetables. Reduce heat to low. Cover; simmer 20 minutes.

4. Stir in chicken and cooked bacon; heat through. Makes about 6 cups or 4 servings.

Easy Paella

This easy and colorful skillet meal is sure to be a hit. Serve with a chilled marinated cucumber salad and French bread. Pictured opposite and on back cover.

1 can (6½ ounces) chopped
    clams
2 tablespoons vegetable oil
8 chicken thighs
    (about 2½ pounds)
1 large onion, chopped
1½ cups regular rice, uncooked
2 cloves garlic, minced

2 cans (10½ ounces *each*)
    Campbell's condensed
    chicken broth
½ teaspoon ground turmeric
½ teaspoon pepper
1 package (10 ounces)
    frozen peas
½ pound medium shrimp,
    shelled and deveined
Lemon wedges

1. Drain clams, reserving liquid. Add enough water to clam liquid to make *1¼ cups;* set aside.

2. In 6-quart Dutch oven over medium-high heat, in hot oil, cook chicken 10 minutes or until browned on all sides. Remove chicken; set aside.

3. Reduce heat to medium. In hot drippings, cook onion, rice and garlic until rice is lightly browned, stirring often. Add reserved clam liquid, broth, turmeric, pepper and chicken. Heat to boiling. Reduce heat to low. Cover; simmer 30 minutes or until chicken is tender and juices run clear.

4. Stir in clams, peas and shrimp. Cover; cook 5 minutes or until shrimp turn pink and opaque. Serve with lemon. Makes 8 servings.

Chicken Stuffing Bake

1 can (10¾ ounces) Campbell's
    condensed cream of
    mushroom soup
1 cup milk
1 package (7 ounces)
    herb-seasoned stuffing mix

2 cups cubed cooked chicken
2 cups cooked broccoli
    flowerets
2 stalks celery, finely chopped
1½ cups shredded Swiss cheese
    (6 ounces), divided

1. Preheat oven to 375°F. Meanwhile, in large bowl, stir soup until smooth. Gradually stir in milk. Add stuffing mix, chicken, broccoli, celery and *1 cup* of the cheese. Spread mixture in greased 12- by 8-inch baking dish.

2. Bake 20 minutes. Top with remaining cheese; bake until cheese melts. Makes 6 servings.

Easy Paella

Country Herbed Chicken

If you like, substitute sliced carrots and quartered cooking onions for the same delicious results. You can also serve with steamed red potatoes as shown in photo. Pictured opposite.

2 tablespoons vegetable oil
2½-to 3-pound broiler-fryer
   chicken, cut up
2 cans (10¾ ounces *each*)
   Campbell's condensed
   creamy chicken mushroom
   soup
½ cup Chablis or other dry
   white wine

2 tablespoons chopped
   fresh parsley
½ teaspoon dried thyme leaves,
   crushed
¼ teaspoon dried rosemary
   leaves, crushed
½ pound whole baby carrots
8 small whole white onions
   Hot cooked red potatoes
   (optional)

1. In 4-quart Dutch oven over medium-high heat, in hot oil, cook chicken 10 minutes or until browned on all sides. Remove chicken; set aside. Spoon off fat.

2. Add next five ingredients. Return chicken to Dutch oven. Heat to boiling. Reduce heat to low. Cover; simmer 15 minutes. Add carrots and onions. Simmer 20 minutes or until chicken is tender and juices run clear. Serve with potatoes, if desired. Makes 4 servings.

Chicken-Broccoli-Rice Skillet

2 tablespoons margarine or
   butter
¾ cup finely chopped carrots
¼ cup chopped green onions
1 pound skinless, boneless
   chicken breasts, cut into
   thin strips

1 can (10¾ ounces) Campbell's
   condensed cream of
   broccoli soup
1 cup milk
⅛ teaspoon pepper
1¼ cups quick-cooking rice,
   uncooked
   Chopped green onions
   for garnish

1. In 10-inch skillet over medium heat, in hot margarine, cook carrots and green onions until tender, stirring occasionally. Push to one side. Add chicken, *half* at a time, cooking until browned on all sides, stirring frequently. Remove chicken as it browns. Return chicken to skillet. Stir in soup, milk and pepper. Heat to boiling. Reduce heat to low. Cover; simmer 10 minutes, stirring occasionally.

2. Stir in rice. Remove from heat. Cover; let stand 5 minutes or until most of liquid is absorbed. Fluff with fork before serving. Garnish with green onions. Makes about 5½ cups or 4 servings.

Country Herbed Chicken

Chicken-Broccoli Cordon Bleu

For Chicken Cordon Bleu, substitute cream of chicken soup for the broccoli soup. Pictured opposite.

2 whole chicken breasts, split, skinned and boned (about 1 pound boneless)

4 thin slices (1 ounce *each*) fully cooked ham

4 thin slices (1 ounce *each*) Swiss cheese

2 tablespoons vegetable oil

1 can (10¾ ounces) Campbell's condensed cream of broccoli soup

⅓ cup milk

¼ cup sliced green onions

⅛ teaspoon dried thyme leaves, crushed

Chopped fresh parsley for garnish

1. Place chicken between 2 pieces of plastic wrap. With meat mallet or rolling pin, pound chicken to ¼-inch thickness. Place a ham slice and cheese slice on *each* breast half. Roll up chicken from narrow end, jelly-roll fashion. Tuck in ham and cheese if necessary; secure with wooden toothpicks.

2. In 10-inch skillet over medium heat, in hot oil, cook chicken 10 minutes or until browned on all sides. Spoon off fat.

3. Stir in soup, milk, green onions and thyme. Heat to boiling. Reduce heat to low. Cover; simmer 10 minutes or until chicken is tender and juices run clear. Garnish with parsley. Makes 4 servings.

To microwave: Omit oil. Prepare chicken rolls as directed in step 1. Place chicken seam-side down in 12- by 8-inch microwave-safe baking dish. Cover with vented plastic wrap; microwave on HIGH 5 minutes. In small bowl, combine soup, milk, green onions and thyme. Pour over chicken. Cover; microwave on HIGH 10 minutes or until chicken is tender and juices run clear, rotating dish halfway through cooking. Let stand, covered, 5 minutes. Garnish as directed in step 3.

> *To save time at the last minute, prepare greens for salads in advance. Rinse greens with cold water and drain. Pat dry with paper towels or spin in salad spinner. Then refrigerate in sealed plastic bag.*

Chicken-Broccoli Cordon Bleu

Tamale Pie

1 pound ground beef
2 teaspoons chili powder
1 can (10¾ ounces) Campbell's
   condensed tomato soup
1 cup coarsely chopped green
   pepper

1 cup whole kernel corn
½ cup salsa
¼ cup water
1 package (8½ to 12 ounces)
   corn muffin mix

1. Preheat oven to 400°F.

2. In 10-inch skillet over medium heat, cook beef and chili powder until beef is browned, stirring to separate meat. Spoon off fat.

3. Stir in soup, green pepper, corn, salsa and water. Heat to boiling. Reduce heat to low. Cover; simmer 5 minutes. Pour into 2-quart casserole. Prepare corn muffin mix according to package directions; spoon evenly over soup mixture.

4. Bake 25 minutes or until a wooden toothpick inserted in center of muffin mixture comes out clean. Makes 6 servings.

> *Save cleanup time—line baking dishes with heavy-duty aluminum foil.*

Macaroni Ratatouille Soup

1 pound sweet Italian sausage,
   casing removed
1 medium onion, chopped
2 cloves garlic, minced
½ teaspoon dried oregano leaves,
   crushed
1 can (10¾ ounces) Campbell's
   condensed tomato soup
1 can (10½ ounces) Campbell's
   condensed beef broth
1 can (8 ounces) tomatoes,
   undrained, cut up

2 cups water
1 pound eggplant, cut into
   ½-inch pieces
½ teaspoon pepper
½ cup elbow macaroni,
   uncooked
Chopped fresh parsley
   for garnish
Grated Parmesan cheese
   for garnish

1. In 5-quart Dutch oven over medium heat, cook sausage, onion, garlic and oregano until sausage is browned, stirring to separate sausage. Spoon off fat.

2. Stir in soup, broth, tomatoes, water, eggplant and pepper. Heat to boiling. Reduce heat to low. Cover; simmer 15 minutes.

3. Stir in macaroni; cook 10 minutes more or until macaroni is tender, stirring occasionally. Garnish with parsley and Parmesan. Makes 7 cups or 5 servings.

Ham Barley Soup

A hearty meal when accompanied with garlic bread or breadsticks.

3 tablespoons margarine
   or butter
1 cup sliced fresh mushrooms
$\frac{1}{2}$ cup chopped onion
$\frac{1}{4}$ teaspoon dried thyme leaves,
   crushed
$\frac{2}{3}$ cup regular pearl barley
1 can (10$\frac{1}{2}$ ounces) Campbell's
   condensed chicken broth

1 can (10$\frac{1}{2}$ ounces) Campbell's
   condensed beef broth
1$\frac{1}{2}$ cups water
$\frac{1}{4}$ teaspoon pepper
1$\frac{1}{2}$ cups milk
$\frac{1}{4}$ pound fully cooked ham, cut
   into 1$\frac{1}{2}$-inch julienne strips
   (1 cup)
1 cup frozen peas

1. In 4-quart saucepan over medium heat, in hot margarine, cook mushrooms, onion and thyme 3 minutes, stirring occasionally. Add barley; cook 2 minutes or until golden, stirring often.

2. Add broths, water and pepper. Cover; heat to boiling. Reduce heat to low. Simmer 40 minutes.

3. Stir in milk, ham and peas. Cook 5 minutes more or until barley is tender. Makes 6$\frac{1}{2}$ cups or 4 servings.

Sausage Stuffing Broccoli Bake

1 package (10 ounces) frozen
   chopped broccoli
$\frac{1}{2}$ pound bulk pork sausage
3 cups plain croutons
2 cups shredded sharp Cheddar
   or Swiss cheese (8 ounces)

1 can (10$\frac{3}{4}$ ounces) Campbell's
   condensed cream of
   broccoli soup
4 eggs
1 soup can milk

1. Preheat oven to 400°F. Cook broccoli according to package directions; drain.

2. Meanwhile, in 10-inch skillet over medium heat, cook sausage until browned, stirring to separate meat. Spoon off fat.

3. In large bowl, combine cooked sausage, cooked broccoli, croutons and cheese; toss lightly to mix. Arrange mixture evenly in greased 12- by 8-inch baking dish.

4. In same bowl, stir soup until smooth. Beat in eggs and milk. Pour over sausage mixture, covering all ingredients. Bake 30 minutes or until set in center. Let stand 10 minutes before serving. Cut into squares to serve. Makes 9 servings.

> *Rely on your microwave oven to thaw frozen vegetables* in minutes for use in a recipe—use the defrost cycle.

Nacho Pork Chili

Serve with hot cornbread sticks and whipped honey butter.
Pictured opposite.

2 tablespoons vegetable oil
1 pound boneless pork shoulder
   or loin roast, cut into
   ³/₄-inch pieces
1 clove garlic, minced
1 tablespoon chili powder
1 teaspoon ground cumin
1 can (11 ounces) Campbell's
   condensed nacho cheese
   soup

1 cup beer
1 can (8 ounces) tomatoes,
   undrained, cut up
1 can (16 ounces) white or red
   kidney beans, drained
Hot cooked rice
Sour cream for garnish
Chopped green onions for
   garnish

1. In 3-quart saucepan over medium heat, in hot oil, cook pork *half* at a time, until browned on all sides, stirring occasionally. Remove pork as it browns. Return pork to saucepan. Add garlic, chili powder and cumin. Cook 5 minutes, stirring occasionally.

2. Stir in soup, beer and tomatoes. Heat to boiling. Reduce heat to low. Cover; simmer 40 minutes or until pork is no longer pink. Add beans. Heat through. Serve chili over rice. Garnish with sour cream and green onions. Makes 4 cups or 4 servings.

German-Style Pork Stew

2 tablespoons vegetable oil
1 pound boneless pork shoulder
   roast, cut into
   ³/₄-inch pieces
2 cans (10³/₄ ounces *each*)
   Campbell's condensed
   cream of celery soup
³/₄ cup apple juice
¹/₂ teaspoon pepper

¹/₂ teaspoon caraway seed
2 medium red potatoes, cut into
   1-inch chunks
¹/₂ cup water
3 cups coarsely chopped
   cabbage
3 medium carrots, diagonally
   sliced
¹/₂ cup milk

1. In 4-quart saucepan over medium heat, in hot oil, cook pork *half* at a time, until browned on all sides, stirring occasionally. Remove pork as it browns.

2. Return pork to saucepan. Stir in soup, juice, pepper and caraway seed. Cover; heat to boiling. Reduce heat to low. Cook 10 minutes, stirring occasionally. Add potatoes and water. Cover; cook 10 minutes. Add cabbage and carrots. Cover; cook 15 minutes or until vegetables are tender and pork is no longer pink. Stir in milk; heat through. Makes 8 cups or 6 servings.

Nacho Pork Chili

Pork Normandy

1 tablespoon vegetable oil
6 pork chops, cut ½ inch thick
    (about 1½ pounds)
1 can (10¾ ounces) Campbells'
    condensed cream of
    mushroom soup
½ cup apple juice

1 medium apple, chopped
½ cup sliced celery
¼ teaspoon dried thyme leaves,
    crushed
Hot cooked noodles
Apple slices for garnish

1. In 10-inch skillet over medium heat, in hot oil, cook chops, *half* at a time, about 10 minutes or until browned on both sides. Spoon off fat.

2. Stir in soup, apple juice, chopped apple, celery and thyme. Heat to boiling. Return chops to skillet. Reduce heat to low. Cover; cook 10 minutes or until chops are no longer pink, stirring occasionally.

3. Serve over hot cooked noodles. Garnish with apple slices. Makes 6 servings.

Winter Lamb Stew

Use beef stew meat instead of lamb if your family prefers. Just increase the cooking time about 20 minutes. Pictured opposite.

1 tablespoon vegetable oil
1 pound boneless lamb shoulder
    roast, cut into
    ¾-inch pieces
½ cup coarsely chopped onion
1 teaspoon paprika
1 can (10¾ ounces) Campbell's
    condensed beefy mushroom
    soup
1 can (8 ounces) tomatoes,
    undrained, cut up

1 soup can water
1 pound butternut or acorn
    squash, peeled, seeded and
    cut into ½-inch pieces
    (about 2 cups)
1 cup whole kernel corn
⅛ teaspoon pepper
2 tablespoons chopped fresh
    parsley

1. In 4-quart saucepan over medium heat, in hot oil, cook lamb *half* at a time, until browned, stirring often. Remove lamb as it browns.

2. In same saucepan over medium heat, cook onion and paprika 2 minutes, stirring occasionally. Stir in soup, tomatoes and water. Return lamb to saucepan. Heat to boiling. Reduce heat to low. Cover; simmer 25 minutes.

3. Add squash, corn and pepper. Cover; cook 15 minutes more or until lamb and vegetables are tender. Stir in parsley. Makes 4 servings.

Winter Lamb Stew

Beef Ziti Casserole

Most any combination of cooked vegetables can be used. It's a terrific way to use leftovers, too.

8 ounces ziti or mostaccioli macaroni, uncooked

2 cups frozen mixed vegetables (zucchini, green beans, carrots)

1 pound ground beef

2 cans (10¾ ounces *each*) Campbell's condensed golden mushroom soup

1 can (8 ounces) tomatoes, undrained, cut up

1 teaspoon dried basil leaves, crushed

¼ teaspoon pepper

⅛ teaspoon garlic powder

1 cup shredded sharp American process cheese (4 ounces)

1. Preheat oven to 400°F. Cook ziti and mixed vegetables according to package directions for *each*; drain. Return cooked ziti and vegetables to cooking pot used to cook ziti.

2. Meanwhile, in 10-inch skillet over medium heat, cook beef until browned, stirring to separate meat. Spoon off fat.

3. Stir in soup, tomatoes, basil, pepper and garlic. Heat through. Add soup mixture to ziti mixture; mix well. Spoon into greased 12- by 8-inch baking dish. Cover with foil; bake 15 minutes.

4. Uncover; sprinkle with cheese. Bake 5 minutes more or until cheese melts. Makes 7½ cups or 6 servings.

Calico Tuna-Rice Bake

Turn to this versatile casserole when time is short. Substitute 1 can (7½ ounces) salmon or 1½ cups cubed, cooked chicken for the tuna, if you like.

⅔ cup regular rice, uncooked

1 can (10¾ ounces) Campbell's condensed cream of celery soup

½ cup milk

1 can (6½ ounces) tuna, drained and flaked

1 cup frozen peas and carrots, thawed

1. Preheat oven to 400°F. Cook rice according to package directions.

2. Meanwhile, in 10- by 6-inch baking dish, combine soup and milk. Add tuna, vegetables and cooked rice; stir gently to mix.

3. Bake 20 minutes or until hot and bubbling; stir. Makes 4 cups or 4 servings.

Meatball 'n' Green Bean Soup

½ pound bulk pork sausage
Vegetable oil
2 medium onions, chopped
2 medium carrots, sliced
1 can (10¾ ounces) Campbell's condensed golden mushroom soup
1 can (10½ ounces) Campbell's condensed chicken broth
2½ cups water
3 medium all-purpose potatoes, cut into ¾-inch pieces
1 cup frozen cut green beans
⅛ teaspoon pepper

1. Shape sausage into 16 (1-inch) meatballs. In 4-quart saucepan over medium heat, brown meatballs on all sides. Remove and drain on paper towels, reserving drippings in pan.

2. Add enough oil to pan drippings to make *1 tablespoon*, if necessary. Over medium heat, in hot drippings, cook onions and carrots 3 minutes. Spoon off fat.

3. Stir in soup, broth, water, potatoes, green beans, pepper and cooked meatballs. Heat to boiling. Reduce heat to low. Cover; cook 10 minutes more or until potatoes and beans are tender. Makes 7½ cups or 5 servings.

Shrimp in Pastry Puffs

For a special touch, sprinkle with a little snipped fresh parsley, chives or watercress.

6 frozen patty shells
2 tablespoons margarine or butter
2 cups sliced fresh mushrooms
1 can (10¾ ounces) Campbell's condensed cream of celery soup
¼ cup Chablis or other dry white wine
½ cup frozen peas
1½ pounds small shrimp, shelled and deveined

1. Preheat oven and bake patty shells according to package directions; keep warm.

2. Meanwhile, in 10-inch skillet over medium heat, in hot margarine, cook mushrooms until tender and liquid is evaporated, stirring occasionally.

3. Stir in soup, wine and peas. Heat to boiling. Stir in shrimp; cook until shrimp turn pink and opaque. Spoon shrimp mixture over patty shells. Makes 5 cups or 6 servings.

Gingered Vegetables

*Some of our taste-testers preferred this served on a bed of rice.
Pictured opposite.*

1 tablespoon vegetable oil
1 cup *each* diagonally sliced
    carrots, diagonally sliced
    celery, sweet red pepper
    strips, coarsely chopped
    onion, broccoli flowerets
    and snow peas

1 clove garlic, minced
½ teaspoon ground ginger
2 tablespoons cornstarch
1 can (10½ ounces) Campbell's
    condensed chicken broth

1. In 10-inch skillet or wok over high heat, in hot oil, stir-fry carrots, celery, red pepper and onion 3 minutes.

2. Add broccoli, snow peas, garlic and ginger. Sprinkle cornstarch over vegetables. Stir in broth. Cook until mixture boils and thickens, stirring often. Reduce heat to low. Cover; simmer until vegetables are tender-crisp.

3. Serve with *soy sauce*, if desired. Makes 4 cups or 4 servings.

To microwave: Omit oil. In 3-quart microwave-safe casserole, combine vegetables and garlic. Cover with lid; microwave on HIGH 7 minutes or until vegetables are tender-crisp, stirring once during cooking. Sprinkle cornstarch over vegetables. Stir in ginger and broth until blended. Cover; microwave on HIGH 4 minutes or until thickened, stirring once during cooking. Serve as directed in step 3.

> *You can reduce the sodium in your meals by using a
> reduced-sodium soy sauce.*

Gingered Vegetables

Curry-Sauced Cauliflower 〰〰

A great make-ahead recipe—just reheat in your microwave oven.
Pictured opposite.

4 cups cauliflowerets
1 can (10¾ ounces) Campbell's
   condensed cream of celery
   soup
½ cup milk
½ cup shredded Cheddar cheese
   (2 ounces)

½ teaspoon curry powder
   Generous dash pepper
1 cup frozen peas, thawed
½ cup diced sweet red pepper
   Toasted sliced almonds
   for garnish

1. In covered 10-inch skillet over medium heat, in ½ inch boiling
   water, cook cauliflower 5 minutes or until tender-crisp. Drain
   in colander.

2. In same skillet, combine soup, milk, cheese, curry and pepper. Add
   cooked cauliflower, peas and red pepper. Over medium heat, cook
   5 minutes or until vegetables are tender, stirring often. Garnish with
   almonds. Makes 5 cups or 10 servings.

To microwave: In 2-quart microwave-safe casserole, place cauliflower
in ½ inch water. Cover with lid; microwave on HIGH 10 minutes or
until tender-crisp. Drain in colander. In same casserole, stir soup, milk,
cheese, curry and pepper until smooth. Add cooked cauliflower, peas
and red pepper. Cover; microwave on HIGH 3 minutes or until
vegetables are tender and cheese melts, stirring once during cooking.
Garnish as directed in step 2.

Vegetables in Two Cheese-Beer Sauce

2 cups broccoli flowerets
2 cups cauliflowerets
1 can (11 ounces) Campbell's
   condensed Cheddar cheese
   soup

⅓ cup beer
1½ cups shredded Swiss cheese
   (6 ounces)
   Dash ground nutmeg

1. In covered 4-quart saucepan over medium heat, in 1 inch boiling
   water, cook broccoli and cauliflower 6 minutes or until tender. Drain
   in colander.

2. Meanwhile, in 2-quart saucepan, combine soup, beer, cheese and
   nutmeg. Over medium heat, heat through, stirring frequently.

3. On serving platter, arrange vegetables alternating broccoli and
   cauliflower to resemble a head of cauliflower. Pour sauce over
   vegetables. Makes 2 cups sauce for vegetables or 6 servings.

Curry-Sauced Cauliflower

Spicy Potatoes Olé

These zesty potatoes taste terrific with broiled poultry or pork.

1 package (24 ounces) frozen
    diced potatoes (5 cups)
2 tablespoons margarine
    or butter
1 cup diced zucchini
1/2 teaspoon chili powder

1 can (11 ounces) Campbell's
    condensed nacho cheese
    soup
1 can (8 ounces) whole kernel
    corn, drained
1/2 cup shredded Monterey Jack
    cheese (2 ounces)

1. In 3-quart saucepan over high heat, heat 1 quart salted water to boiling. Add potatoes. Return to boiling. Cook 2 minutes or until potatoes are tender. Drain in colander, reserving 1/2 *cup* of the cooking liquid; set aside.

2. In same saucepan over medium heat, in hot margarine, cook zucchini and chili powder 2 minutes, stirring often.

3. Stir in soup, corn, cheese, cooked potatoes and reserved 1/2 *cup* liquid. Cook 5 minutes or until heated through, stirring often. Serve with *sour cream*, if desired. Makes 6 cups or 8 servings.

To microwave: In 2-quart microwave-safe casserole, combine potatoes and margarine. Cover with lid; microwave on HIGH 6 minutes or until potatoes are tender, stirring once during heating. Stir in zucchini, chili powder, soup and corn. Cover; microwave on HIGH 5 minutes or until vegetables are tender. Sprinkle with cheese. Let stand, uncovered, 2 minutes. Serve as directed in step 3.

Quick Rice and Beans

3 slices bacon, diced
1 clove garlic, minced
1/4 teaspoon ground coriander
1/8 teaspoon ground cumin
1 cup regular rice, uncooked
1/2 cup drained canned chick
    peas (garbanzo beans),
    kidney beans or pinto beans

1 can (10 1/2 ounces) Campbell's
    condensed beef broth
1/2 cup water
1 bay leaf
    Generous dash pepper

1. In 2-quart saucepan over medium-high heat, cook bacon until crisp. Add garlic, coriander and cumin. Cook 1 minute, stirring constantly.

2. Stir in rice, chick peas, broth, water, bay leaf and pepper. Heat to boiling. Reduce heat to low. Cover; simmer 20 minutes or until rice is done. Remove bay leaf; discard. Makes 4 cups or 8 servings.

Broccoli-Rice Casserole 〰〰

Serve at a family picnic or neighborhood potluck.

1 tablespoon vegetable oil
½ cup chopped celery
¼ cup chopped onion
1 can (10¾ ounces) Campbell's
   condensed cream of broccoli
   or cream of mushroom soup
¼ cup milk
1 cup pasteurized process
   cheese spread cut in
   ¼-inch cubes

1 package (10 ounces) frozen
   chopped broccoli, thawed
   and drained
1 can (8 ounces) sliced water
   chestnuts, drained
2 cups cooked regular rice
   Paprika

1. Preheat oven to 350°F. In 1½-quart saucepan over medium heat, in hot oil, cook celery and onion until tender-crisp, stirring occasionally. Stir in soup and milk.

2. In 10- by 6-inch baking dish, place cheese, broccoli, water chestnuts and rice. Stir in soup mixture. Sprinkle with paprika. Bake 30 minutes or until bubbling. Makes 5 cups or 8 servings.

To microwave: Omit oil. In 10- by 6-inch microwave-safe baking dish, combine celery and onion. Cover with vented plastic wrap; microwave on HIGH 3 minutes. Stir in soup and milk. Add cheese, broccoli, water chestnuts and rice, stirring gently to mix. Sprinkle with paprika. Microwave, uncovered, on HIGH 10 minutes, rotating dish halfway through cooking.

Squash 'n' Macaroni in Spicy Cheese Sauce

6 ounces corkscrew macaroni,
   uncooked
2 tablespoons margarine
   or butter
4 cups sliced zucchini or yellow
   squash
¼ cup sliced green onions
1 clove garlic, minced

½ teaspoon ground cumin
1 can (11 ounces) Campbell's
   condensed Cheddar cheese
   soup
½ cup milk
½ cup shredded Cheddar cheese
   (2 ounces)

1. Cook macaroni according to package directions; drain. In 3-quart saucepan over medium heat, in hot margarine, cook squash, green onions, garlic and cumin 5 minutes or until squash is tender-crisp, stirring often.

2. Stir in soup, milk and cheese. Heat until cheese melts. Stir in drained macaroni; heat through. Makes 6 cups or 6 servings.

Peas and Carrots in Thyme Sauce

Even kids will love this sophisticated version of peas and carrots. Serve with mini hamburgers as shown. Pictured opposite.

1 tablespoon margarine
   or butter
1 small onion, chopped
¼ teaspoon dried thyme leaves,
   crushed
1 can (10¾ ounces) Campbell's
   condensed cream of celery
   soup

⅓ cup milk
   Generous dash pepper
1 bag (16 ounces) frozen peas
1 cup carrots cut into 2-inch
   julienne strips

1. In 2-quart saucepan over medium heat, in hot margarine, cook onion and thyme until onion is tender, stirring occasionally.

2. Stir in soup, milk and pepper. Add peas and carrots. Heat to boiling. Reduce heat to low. Cover; simmer 8 minutes or until vegetables are tender, stirring occasionally. Makes 3½ cups or 4 servings.

Broccoli Bake

2 packages (10 ounces *each*)
   frozen broccoli spears or 1
   package (20 ounces) frozen
   broccoli cuts
1 can (10¾ ounces) Campbell's
   condensed cream of broccoli
   or cream of mushroom soup

½ cup milk
1 teaspoon soy sauce
   Dash pepper
1 can (2.8 ounces) French-
   fried onions, divided

1. Preheat oven to 350°F. Cook broccoli according to package directions; drain.

2. Meanwhile, in small bowl, combine soup, milk, soy sauce and pepper. In 10- by 6-inch baking dish, layer *half* of the broccoli, *half* of the soup mixture and *half* of the onions. Top with remaining broccoli and the soup mixture. Bake 25 minutes.

3. Top with remaining onions. Bake 5 minutes more. Makes 6 servings.

To microwave: Prepare as directed *except* use a 10- by 6-inch microwave-safe baking dish. Cover with waxed paper; microwave on HIGH 8 minutes, rotating dish halfway through heating. Top with remaining onions. Microwave, uncovered, on HIGH 1 minute more.

Peas and Carrots in Thyme Sauce

Mixed Vegetable Pilaf

Pictured opposite along with ham, cranberry sauce and green beans.

2 tablespoons margarine
   or butter
1 cup sliced fresh mushrooms
¼ teaspoon dried basil leaves,
   crushed
1 can (10½ ounces) Campbell's
   condensed chicken broth

¾ cup water
1 cup regular rice, uncooked
1 small zucchini, halved
   lengthwise and sliced
½ cup shredded carrot

1. In 10-inch skillet over medium heat, in hot margarine, cook mushrooms and basil 3 minutes, stirring occasionally.

2. Add broth and water. Heat to boiling. Stir in rice. Return to boiling. Reduce heat to low. Cover; simmer 15 minutes.

3. Stir in zucchini and carrot. Cover; simmer 5 minutes. Remove from heat. Let stand, covered, 5 minutes before serving. Makes about 5 cups or 6 servings.

Mushrooms in Garlic-Herb Sauce

Toss with hot cooked pasta or spooned over grilled meats.

2 tablespoons olive oil
1 medium onion, finely
   chopped
4 cloves garlic, minced
¼ teaspoon dried rosemary
   leaves, crushed
¼ teaspoon dried thyme leaves,
   crushed
1½ pounds fresh mushrooms,
   thinly sliced

1 can (10½ ounces) Campbell's
   condensed French onion
   soup
1 teaspoon lime or lemon juice
¼ cup Chablis or other dry
   white wine
Chopped fresh parsley for
   garnish

1. In 10-inch skillet over medium heat, in hot oil, cook onion, garlic, rosemary and thyme until onion is tender, stirring occasionally.

2. Increase heat to medium-high. Add mushrooms. Cook until mushrooms just begin to brown, stirring occasionally. Add soup and lime juice. Heat to boiling. Reduce heat to low. Simmer until mushrooms are just tender, stirring occasionally.

3. Add wine. Simmer 3 minutes. Garnish with parsley. Makes 2¾ cups or 6 servings.

Mixed Vegetable Pilaf

Cheese-Sauced Summer Vegetables

Look for fresh sugar snap peas when in season—they cook to perfection in only 5 minutes.

3 tablespoons margarine
    or butter
1 medium zucchini or yellow
    squash, halved lengthwise
    and sliced
1 cup sliced fresh mushrooms
1 clove garlic, minced
¼ teaspoon dried basil leaves,
    crushed

1 can (11 ounces) Campbell's
    condensed Cheddar cheese
    soup
½ cup milk
1 package (8 ounces) frozen
    sugar snap peas (2 cups)
⅛ teaspoon pepper
1 cup cherry tomatoes *each*
    cut in half

1. In 3-quart saucepan over medium heat, in hot margarine, cook zucchini 2 minutes, stirring occasionally. Transfer to bowl.

2. In same saucepan over medium heat, cook mushrooms, garlic and basil 2 minutes, stirring occasionally.

3. Stir soup and milk into saucepan. Add peas and pepper. Heat to boiling. Reduce heat to low. Cover; simmer 5 minutes or until peas are tender, stirring often.

4. Stir in tomatoes and cooked zucchini. Heat through. Makes 4 cups or 6 servings.

Curried Peanut Rice

Just the right accompaniment to your favorite Chinese stir-fry.

2 tablespoons vegetable oil
¼ cup sliced green onions
2 teaspoons curry powder
1 can (10½ ounces) Campbell's
    condensed chicken broth

½ cup frozen peas
1¼ cups quick-cooking rice,
    uncooked
½ cup coarsely chopped
    unsalted roasted peanuts

1. In 2-quart saucepan over medium heat, in hot oil, cook green onions and curry powder until onions are tender, stirring occasionally.

2. Add broth and peas. Heat to boiling. Add rice. Remove from heat. Cover; let stand 5 minutes or until most of the liquid is absorbed. Stir in peanuts. Fluff with fork before serving. Makes 2½ cups or 5 servings.

Savory Parslied Rice

For a spicier rice, stir in a chopped seeded jalapeño pepper
and use the whole can of green chilies.

1 tablespoon margarine
   or butter
½ cup finely chopped onion
2 cloves garlic, minced
1 can (10½ ounces) Campbell's
   condensed chicken broth

1¼ cups quick-cooking rice,
   uncooked
3 tablespoons chopped
   green chilies
¼ cup chopped fresh parsley

1. In 2-quart saucepan over medium heat, in hot margarine, cook
   onion and garlic until onion is tender, stirring occasionally.

2. Add broth. Heat to boiling. Add rice and green chilies. Remove
   from heat. Cover; let stand 5 minutes or until most of the liquid
   is absorbed. Stir in parsley. Fluff with fork before serving. Makes
   3 cups or 6 servings.

Vegetable Couscous

Reheat leftover vegetable couscous in your microwave oven.
Stir in 1 or 2 tablespoons water, if needed.

1 can (10½ ounces) Campbell's
   condensed chicken broth
1½ cups couscous, uncooked
¼ cup vegetable oil
1 cup sliced fresh mushrooms
1 cup chopped onions

1 cup shredded carrots
1 tablespoon grated fresh ginger
2 cloves garlic, minced
1 tablespoon soy sauce
1 tablespoon lemon juice

1. In 2-quart saucepan over high heat, heat broth to boiling. Remove
   from heat. Stir in couscous. Cover; let stand 5 minutes.

2. Meanwhile, in 10-inch skillet over medium heat, in hot oil, cook
   mushrooms, onions, carrots, ginger and garlic until vegetables are
   tender-crisp, stirring often. Stir in soy sauce and lemon juice.

3. Add couscous. Heat through. Makes 5 cups or 10 servings.

Bulgur with Basil and Walnuts

If fresh basil is available, finely chop enough to make 1 tablespoon and stir in with the walnuts.

1 can (10½ ounces) Campbell's
   condensed chicken broth
1 medium onion, chopped
2 tablespoons margarine
   or butter
1 clove garlic, minced

1 teaspoon dried basil leaves,
   crushed
1¼ cups bulgur wheat, uncooked
⅓ cup chopped walnuts
1 tablespoon lemon juice

1. In 2-quart saucepan over medium heat, combine broth, onion, margarine, garlic and basil. Heat to boiling.

2. Add remaining ingredients. Remove from heat. Cover; let stand 15 minutes or until liquid is absorbed. Makes about 4 cups or 8 servings.

Summer Garden Soup

If fresh basil isn't available, use ½ teaspoon crushed dried basil— just add it before the soup simmers. Pictured opposite.

1 can (10½ ounces) Campbell's
   condensed chicken broth
⅔ cup water
½ cup zucchini cut in 2-inch
   julienne strips
½ cup seeded and chopped
   tomato

½ cup frozen whole kernel corn
⅓ cup chopped carrot
¼ cup chopped onion
1½ teaspoons chopped fresh
   basil leaves

In 2-quart saucepan over high heat, combine all ingredients *except* fresh basil. Heat to boiling. Reduce heat to low. Simmer 10 minutes or until vegetables are tender, stirring occasionally. Stir in basil. Makes 3 cups or 3 servings.

To microwave: In 1½-quart microwave-safe casserole, combine all ingredients *except* fresh basil. Cover with lid; microwave on HIGH 12 minutes or until vegetables are tender, stirring twice during cooking. Stir in basil.

Summer Garden Soup

Quick Gazpacho

Tomato soup is the base for this fast-fixin' soup. Pictured opposite.

1 can (10¾ ounces) Campbell's
condensed tomato soup
1 soup can water
1 tablespoon wine vinegar
1 teaspoon olive oil
1 clove garlic, minced
¼ teaspoon dried basil leaves,
crushed

1 cup seeded and chopped
cucumber
½ cup chopped sweet red or
green pepper
1 tablespoon chopped onion
Fresh basil leaves for garnish

1. In medium bowl, stir soup until smooth. Stir in water, vinegar, oil, garlic and dried basil; blend well. Stir in cucumber, red pepper and onion. Cover; refrigerate until serving time, at least 6 hours.

2. Serve in chilled bowls. Garnish with fresh basil. Makes 3½ cups or 4 servings.

Hint-of-Mint Pea Soup

Fresh mint can be easily grown in your kitchen window.

1 can (10¾ ounces) Campbell's
condensed cream of potato
soup
1 can (10½ ounces) Campbell's
condensed chicken broth
1 package (10 ounces) frozen
peas
1 tablespoon lemon juice

¼ teaspoon dried mint leaves,
crushed, or ¾ teaspoon
chopped fresh mint leaves
⅛ teaspoon ground white pepper
½ cup milk
Fresh mint leaves for garnish
Chopped walnuts for garnish

1. In 2-quart saucepan, combine soup and broth, stirring until smooth. Add peas. Over medium heat, heat to boiling. Reduce heat to low. Cover; simmer 8 minutes or until peas are tender.

2. In covered blender or food processor, blend soup mixture, lemon juice, ¼ teaspoon dried mint and the pepper until smooth. Return mixture to saucepan.

3. Gradually stir in milk. Over medium heat, heat through. Garnish with fresh mint and walnuts. Makes 4 cups or 4 servings.

Quick Gazpacho

Watercress Potato Soup

This is also delicious served cold like classic vichyssoise. Just refrigerate at least 4 hours before serving.

1 tablespoon margarine
or butter
½ cup chopped onion
2 cups chopped watercress
1½ cups water

1 can (10¾ ounces) Campbell's
condensed cream of potato
soup
⅛ teaspoon ground nutmeg
Watercress for garnish

1. In 1½-quart saucepan over medium heat, in hot margarine, cook onion and watercress until onion is tender, stirring occasionally. Add water. Heat to boiling. Reduce heat to low. Cover; simmer 10 minutes. Drain mixture, reserving liquid. Set aside.

2. In covered blender or food processor, blend watercress mixture until almost smooth. Add soup; blend until smooth. Add reserved liquid and nutmeg; blend until smooth. Return to saucepan; heat through. Garnish with watercress. Makes 3 cups or 4 servings.

South-of-the-Border Onion Soup   *EXTRA EASY*

For added zip, top this speedy soup with a spoonful of sour cream and some shredded Monterey Jack cheese with chilies.

1 can (10½ ounces) Campbell's
condensed French onion
soup
1 soup can water
½ cup whole kernel corn

½ cup chopped seeded tomato
2 tablespoons chopped green
chilies
1 tablespoon lime juice
¼ teaspoon ground cumin

In 2-quart saucepan, combine all ingredients. Over medium heat, heat to boiling. Reduce heat to low. Simmer 10 minutes. Makes 4 cups or 4 servings.

Southwest Potato Soup

1 tablespoon margarine
   or butter
½ cup chopped green onions
1 can (10¾ ounces) Campbell's
   condensed cream of potato
   soup
	1½ cups milk
	¼ cup shredded Monterey Jack
	   cheese with chilies
	   (1 ounce)

1. In 2-quart saucepan over medium heat, in hot margarine, cook green onions until tender, stirring occasionally.

2. Add soup and milk; stir until blended. Heat through. Remove from heat. Add cheese, stirring until cheese melts. Makes about 2¾ cups or 3 servings.

Double Clam Chowder

1 can (10¾ ounces) Campbell's
   condensed cream of celery
   soup
1 can (10¾ ounces) Campbell's
   condensed New England
   clam chowder
	1 can (6½ ounces) chopped
	   clams, undrained
	1 soup can milk
	1 soup can water
	   Chopped fresh parsley
	   for garnish

In 2-quart saucepan over medium heat, combine all ingredients *except* parsley. Heat through, stirring occasionally. *Do not boil.* Garnish with parsley. Makes about 5½ cups or 5 servings.

Down-Home Vegetable Chowder

For added flavor, sprinkle crumbled bacon, chopped green onion tops and chopped sweet red pepper on each serving.

2 tablespoons margarine
   or butter
¼ cup sliced green onions
½ cup sliced celery
1 can (10¾ ounces) Campbell's
   condensed cream of
   potato soup
	1 soup can milk
	1 cup frozen whole kernel corn
	⅛ teaspoon pepper

In 2-quart saucepan over medium heat, in hot margarine, cook green onions and celery until tender, stirring occasionally. Add soup, milk, corn and pepper. Heat through, stirring often. Makes 3½ cups or 3 servings.

Dilled Salmon Dip

Look for mini zucchini, eggplant and summer squash to add to your assortment of fresh vegetable dippers. Pictured opposite.

1 can (10¾ ounces) Campbell's condensed cream of celery soup
¼ cup mayonnaise or sour cream
2 tablespoons prepared horseradish

1 tablespoon chopped fresh dill or 1 teaspoon dried dill weed, crushed
⅛ teaspoon pepper
1 can (7½ ounces) salmon, drained and flaked
Fresh chopped dill and dill sprig for garnish

1. In medium bowl, combine soup, mayonnaise, horseradish, 1 tablespoon chopped dill and the pepper; mix well. Add salmon; mix lightly. Cover; chill 15 minutes.

2. Garnish dip as desired. Serve with *assorted cut-up vegetables* and *party rye bread* for dipping. Makes 2 cups.

Middle Eastern-Style Dip

1 can (15 ounces) chick peas (garbanzo beans), drained
1 can (10¾ ounces) Campbell's condensed cream of celery soup
½ cup chopped blanched almonds, toasted

3 tablespoons lemon juice
2 cloves garlic, minced
1 tablespoon olive oil
Generous dash ground red pepper

In covered blender or food processor, combine all ingredients. Blend until smooth. Serve at room temperature or chilled with *pita bread, cut-up fresh vegetables* or *crackers* for dipping. Makes 2¼ cups.

> ***To toast chopped almonds in microwave oven,*** *spread in a single layer on a plain white paper towel. Microwave on HIGH 1½ minutes, stirring once during cooking.*

Dilled Salmon Dip

Curried Peanut Dip

1 can (10¾ ounces) Campbell's
   condensed cream of chicken
   soup
¾ cup plain yogurt

¼ cup chunky peanut butter
2 teaspoons curry powder
   Chopped peanuts for garnish

In small bowl, combine all ingredients. Serve at room temperature or chilled. Garnish with peanuts. Serve with wedges of *fresh pears* and *apples* for dipping. Makes 2 cups.

> *To keep fruit, such as pears and apples, from browning, dip into lemon juice or ascorbic acid color keeper after cutting.*

Artichoke-Chili Dip

Our souper version of the popular hot artichoke dip that's made with mayonnaise.

1 can (10¾ ounces) Campbell's
   condensed cream of celery
   soup
2 packages (3 ounces *each*)
   cream cheese, softened
1 can (14 ounces) artichoke
   hearts, rinsed, drained
   and chopped

1 can (4 ounces) chopped
   green chilies
½ cup grated Parmesan cheese
   Paprika

1. Preheat oven to 375°F.

2. Meanwhile, in 1-quart casserole, stir soup and cream cheese until smooth. Stir in artichokes, chilies and Parmesan. Sprinkle with paprika.

3. Bake 15 minutes or until hot and bubbling. Serve with *crackers* or *tortilla chips* for dipping. Makes 3½ cups.

To microwave: In 1½-quart microwave-safe casserole, stir soup and cream cheese until smooth. Stir in artichokes, chilies and Parmesan. Microwave, uncovered, on HIGH 6 minutes or until hot, stirring twice during cooking. Sprinkle with paprika. Serve as directed in step 3.

Hot Cheese and Sausage Dip

For added zip, use hot Italian sausage.

¼ pound Italian sausage, casing removed, bulk pork sausage or ground raw turkey
⅓ cup chopped green onions

1 can (11 ounces) Campbell's condensed Cheddar cheese soup
½ cup water
Chopped green onions for garnish

1. In 1½-quart saucepan over medium heat, cook sausage and green onions 4 minutes or until sausage is browned, stirring to separate meat. Spoon off fat.

2. Stir in soup and water. Heat until hot and bubbling, stirring occasionally. Pour into heated serving dish or fondue pot. Garnish with green onions. Serve with *celery sticks, carrot sticks, bagel chips* or *tortilla chips* for dipping. Makes about 2 cups.

Potato Skin Nachos

2 packages (20 ounces *each*) frozen potato skins
1 can (11 ounces) Campbell's condensed nacho cheese soup

¼ cup milk
½ cup sliced pitted ripe olives
½ cup chopped sweet red pepper or seeded tomato
¼ cup chopped green onions

1. Prepare frozen potato skins according to package directions; keep warm.

2. Meanwhile, in 1½-quart saucepan over medium heat, combine soup and milk. Heat through, stirring occasionally.

3. Spoon sauce over prepared potato skins. Sprinkle with olives, red pepper and green onions. Makes about 24 appetizers.

Cheddar Swiss Fondue

Along with the bread dippers, serve assorted fresh fruit.
Pictured opposite.

1 tablespoon margarine
   or butter
½ cup chopped onion
1 clove garlic, minced
1 can (11 ounces) Campbell's
   condensed Cheddar cheese
   soup

¼ cup Chablis or other dry
   white wine
1 teaspoon caraway seed
2 cups shredded Swiss cheese
   (8 ounces)

1. In 2-quart saucepan over medium heat, in hot margarine, cook
   onion and garlic 10 minutes, stirring often.

2. Stir in soup, wine and caraway seed. Gradually add cheese, stirring
   until smooth after each addition.

3. Pour cheese mixture into heated serving dish or fondue pot. Serve
   with *pumpernickel* or *French bread cubes* for dipping. Makes
   2⅓ cups.

To microwave: In 2-quart microwave-safe casserole, combine
margarine, onion and garlic. Cover with lid; microwave on HIGH 3 to
4 minutes or until onion is tender, stirring once. Stir in soup, wine,
caraway seed and cheese. Cover; microwave on HIGH 4 to 6 minutes
or until cheese melts, stirring twice during cooking. Serve as directed
in step 3.

Souper-Easy Cheese Dip

1 can (11 ounces) Campbell's
   condensed Cheddar cheese
   soup

2 tablespoons chili sauce
2 tablespoons milk

In 1-quart saucepan, combine all ingredients; mix well. Over medium
heat, heat until mixture is smooth, stirring often. Serve dip with *corn
chips* or as a topper over *French-fried potatoes or potato skins.*
Makes 1¼ cups.

To microwave: In 1-quart microwave-safe casserole, combine all
ingredients; stir well. Cover with lid; microwave on HIGH 4 minutes
or until hot, stirring twice during heating. Serve as directed above.

Cheddar Swiss Fondue

Mini Broccoli Pizzas

These individual broccoli pizzas are easy to assemble. Choose from a variety of toppers such as: sliced pepperoni, chopped artichoke hearts, chopped shrimp, sliced green onions and sliced olives. Pictured opposite and on back cover.

2 cups small broccoli flowerets
½ cup sweet red pepper cut
   in strips
1 can (10¾ ounces) Campbell's
   condensed cream of
   broccoli soup
¼ teaspoon garlic powder

¼ teaspoon dried Italian
   seasoning, crushed
6 English muffins, split
   and toasted
2 cups shredded mozzarella
   cheese (8 ounces)

1. Preheat oven to 375°F.

2. Meanwhile, in small saucepan over high heat, in boiling water, cook broccoli and red pepper 3 minutes. Drain well; set aside.

3. In small bowl, combine soup, garlic and Italian seasoning. Spread soup mixture evenly over 12 muffin halves; place on baking sheets. Top each with cooked broccoli and red pepper. Sprinkle with cheese. Bake 10 minutes or until cheese melts. Serve immediately. Makes 12 mini pizzas.

Cheese 'n' Crab Appetizers

1 can (11 ounces) Campbell's
   condensed Cheddar cheese
   soup
2 tablespoons chopped green
   onion
1 tablespoon chopped pimento

1 teaspoon Louisiana-style
   hot sauce
2 cans (6 ounces *each*) crab
   meat, drained
6 English muffins, split
   and toasted

1. In medium bowl, combine soup, green onion, pimento and hot sauce. Fold in crab meat. Spread soup mixture evenly over 12 muffin halves; place on baking sheets.

2. Broil 6 inches from heat 5 to 6 minutes or until hot and lightly browned. Quarter each muffin half for appetizers or serve as 12 open-face sandwiches. Makes 48 appetizers or 12 open-face sandwiches.

Mini Broccoli Pizzas

FOOD EQUIVALENTS CHART

Bread and Cookies

2 slices bread	1 cup soft bread crumbs
2 slices bread	1 cup bread cubes
14 square graham crackers	1 cup fine crumbs
22 vanilla wafers	1 cup fine crumbs

Dairy

1 pound margarine or butter	2 cups or 4 sticks
1 cup heavy or whipping cream	2 cups whipped
8 ounces cream cheese	1 cup
1 pound Swiss or Cheddar cheese	4 cups shredded
4 ounces blue cheese, crumbled	1 cup
4 ounces Parmesan or Romano cheese	1¼ cups grated
1 large egg	3 tablespoons egg

Dried legumes

1 cup dried beans or peas	2¼ cups cooked

Fruit

1 pound apples	3 medium
1 pound bananas	3 medium
1 medium lemon	2 tablespoons juice
1 medium orange	⅓ to ½ cup juice

Herbs

1 tablespoon fresh	1 teaspoon dried

Pasta

8 ounces elbow macaroni, uncooked	4 cups cooked
8 ounces spaghetti, uncooked	4 cups cooked
8 ounces medium noodles, uncooked	3¾ cups cooked

Rice

1 cup regular long-grain rice, uncooked	3 cups cooked
1 cup quick-cooking rice, uncooked	2 cups cooked

Vegetables

1 pound carrots	2½ cups sliced
1 pound cabbage	4 cups shredded
1 pound onions (yellow)	5 to 6 medium
1 medium onion	½ cup chopped
1 pound all-purpose potatoes	3 medium
1 pound fresh mushrooms	3 cups sliced
1 pound tomatoes	3 medium
1 pound broccoli	2 cups flowerets

Miscellaneous

1 pound cooked meat	3 cups diced
1 pound raw boneless meat	2 cups cooked, cubed
1 pound raw ground beef	2¾ cups cooked

Anise Beef and Rice, 44
Appetizers (*see also* **Dips**)
  Cheese 'n' Crab Appetizers, 92
  Mini Broccoli Pizzas, 92
  Potato Skin Nachos, 89
Artichoke-Chili Dip, 88

Bacon Mac Skillet, Bean-and-, 41
Barley Soup, Ham, 61
Bavarian Kielbasa with Noodles, 46
Bean-and-Bacon Mac Skillet, 41
Beef (*see also* **Ground Beef**)
  Anise Beef and Rice, 44
  Garlic Orange Beef, 40
  Philadelphia Cheesesteak Soup, 25
  Reuben-Style Skillet, 17
  Spicy Broccoli Beef, 12
Beef Ziti Casserole, 66
Broccoli Bake, 74
Broccoli Chicken Dijon, 32
Broccoli Fish Chowder, 29
Broccoli-Rice Casserole, 73
Bulgur with Basil and Walnuts, 80

Cabbage Soup, Hearty Sausage 'n', 49
Calico Tuna-Rice Bake, 66
Cauliflower, Curry-Sauced, 70
Cheddar Swiss Fondue, 90
Cheese
  Bean-and-Bacon Mac Skillet, 41
  Cheddar Swiss Fondue, 90
  Cheese 'n' Crab Appetizers, 92
  Cheese-Sauced Summer Vegetables, 78
  Cheesy Mushroom Frittata, 46
  Cheesy Tuna and Twists, 29
  Chicken-Broccoli Cordon Bleu, 58
  Fish with Swiss Cheese Sauce, 28
  Mini Broccoli Pizzas, 92
  Potato Skin Nachos, 89
  Reuben-Style Skillet, 17
  Squash 'n' Macaroni in Spicy Cheese Sauce, 73
  Vegetables in Two Cheese-Beer Sauce, 70
Cheeseburger Pizza, 38
Chicken (*see also* **Turkey**)
  Broccoli Chicken Dijon, 32
  Chicken 'n' Shrimp Gumbo, 24
  Chicken-Broccoli Cordon Bleu, 58
  Chicken-Broccoli Divan, 9
  Chicken-Broccoli-Rice Skillet, 56
  Chicken Enchiladas, 52
  Chicken in Spicy Peanut Sauce, 34
  Chicken Pineapple Stir-Fry, 34

Chicken Stuffing Bake, 54
Chicken with Julienne Vegetables, 32
Classic Glorified Chicken, 52
Country Herbed Chicken, 56
Country-Style Smothered Chicken, 53
Curried Chicken Vegetable Chowder, 30
Easy Basil Chicken with Rice, 10
Easy Paella, 54
Garden-Style Vegetable Bisque, 36
Lemon-Broccoli Chicken, 30
Mandarin Chicken, 35
Nacho Chicken Tostadas, 10
Shortcut Brunswick Stew, 53
Souper Chicken Tetrazzini, 35
Cincinnati Chili, 41
Classic Campbelled Eggs, 16
Classic Glorified Chicken, 52
Cod Steaks Oriental, 14
Country Ham 'n' Potato Soup, 25
Country Herbed Chicken, 56
Country-Style Smothered Chicken, 53
Couscous, Vegetable, 79
Creamy Dill Salmon Steaks, 28
Creamy Shrimp Bisque, 20
Curried Chicken-Vegetable Chowder, 30
Curried Peanut Dip, 88
Curried Peanut Rice, 78
Curry-Sauced Cauliflower, 70

Dijon Cod Fillets, 27
Dilled Salmon Dip, 87
Dips (*see also* **Appetizers**)
  Artichoke-Chili Dip, 88
  Cheddar Swiss Fondue, 90
  Curried Peanut Dip, 88
  Dilled Salmon Dip, 87
  Hot Cheese and Sausage Dip, 89
  Middle Eastern-Style Dip, 87
  Souper-Easy Cheese Dip, 90
Double Clam Chowder, 85
Down-Home Vegetable Chowder, 85

Easy Basil Chicken with Rice, 10
Easy Creole Soup, 36
Easy Paella, 54
Easy Turkey Salad, 18
Eggs
  Cheesy Mushroom Frittata, 46
  Classic Campbelled Eggs, 16
  Fiesta Eggs, 48
  Sausage Stuffing Broccoli Bake, 61

Fettuccine with Mushroom-Clam Sauce, 14
Fiesta Eggs, 48
Fish
  Broccoli Fish Chowder, 29
  Calico Tuna-Rice Bake, 66
  Cheesy Tuna and Twists, 29
  Cod Steaks Oriental, 14
  Creamy Dill Salmon Steaks, 28
  Dijon Cod Fillets, 27
  Dilled Salmon Dip, 87
  Fish with Swiss Cheese Sauce, 28
  Salsa Swordfish, 27
  Tuna-Tortellini Soup, 20
Food Equivalents Chart, 94

Garden-Style Vegetable Bisque, 36
Garlic Orange Beef, 40
German-Style Pork Stew, 62
Gingered Vegetables, 69
Ground Beef
  Beef Ziti Casserole, 66
  Cheeseburger Pizza, 38
  Cincinnati Chili, 41
  Hamburger 'n' Fixings Sandwiches, 17
  Hearty Sausage 'n' Cabbage Soup, 49
  Meatball Mushroom Sandwiches, 38
  Pineapple Beef Curry, 42
  Southwest Mac and Beef, 42
  Speedy Spicy Chili, 13
  Taco Salad, 44
  Tamale Pie, 60

Ham
  Chicken-Broccoli Cordon Bleu, 58
  Country Ham 'n' Potato Soup, 25
  Ham Barley Soup, 61
Hamburger 'n' Fixings Sandwiches, 17
Hearty Sausage 'n' Cabbage Soup, 49
Hint-of-Mint Pea Soup, 82
Hot Cheese and Sausage Dip, 89

Knockwurst Potato Chowder, 22

Lamb Stew, Winter, 64
Lemon-Broccoli Chicken, 30

Macaroni Ratatouille Soup, 60
Mandarin Chicken, 35
Meatball 'n' Green Bean Soup, 67
Meatball Mushroom Sandwiches, 38
Middle Eastern-Style Dip, 87
Mini Broccoli Pizzas, 92
Mixed Vegetable Pilaf, 76
Mushrooms in Garlic-Herb Sauce, 76

Nacho Chicken Tostadas, 10
Nacho Pork Chili, 62

Pasta
Bavarian Kielbasa with Noodles, 46
Bean-and-Bacon Mac Skillet, 41
Beef Ziti Casserole, 66
Cheesy Tuna and Twists, 29
Fettuccine with Mushroom-Clam
Sauce, 14
Macaroni Ratatouille Soup, 60
Saucy Cheese Tortellini, 16
Souper Chicken Tetrazzini, 35
Southwest Mac and Beef, 42
Squash 'n' Macaroni in Spicy Cheese
Sauce, 73
Tuna-Tortellini Soup, 20
Peas and Carrots in Thyme Sauce, 74
Pepperoni Pizza Soup, 18
Philadelphia Cheesesteak Soup, 25
Pineapple Beef Curry, 42
Piquant Pork Chops, 40

Pork
German-Style Pork Stew, 62
Nacho Pork Chili, 62
Piquant Pork Chops, 40
Pork Normandy, 64
Skillet Black-Eyed Peas 'n' Rice, 12
Szechuan Shredded Pork, 13
Potato Skin Nachos, 89

Quick Gazpacho, 82
Quick Rice and Beans, 72

Reuben-Style Skillet, 17

Salsa Swordfish, 27

Sandwiches
Cheeseburger Pizza, 38
Hamburger 'n' Fixings Sandwiches, 17
Meatball Mushroom Sandwiches, 38
Mini Broccoli Pizzas, 92
Saucy Cheese Tortellini, 16

Sausage
Bavarian Kielbasa with Noodles, 46
Hearty Sausage 'n' Cabbage Soup, 49
Hot Cheese and Sausage Dip, 89
Knockwurst Potato Chowder, 22
Macaroni Ratatouille Soup, 60
Meatball 'n' Green Bean Soup, 67
Meatball Mushroom Sandwiches, 38
Pepperoni Pizza Soup, 18
Sausage Skillet Dinner, 49
Sausage Stuffing Broccoli Bake, 61
Savory Parslied Rice, 79

Shellfish
Cheese 'n' Crab Appetizers, 92
Chicken 'n' Shrimp Gumbo, 24
Creamy Shrimp Bisque, 20
Double Clam Chowder, 85
Easy Creole Soup, 36
Easy Paella, 54
Fettuccine with Mushroom-Clam
Sauce, 14
Shrimp in Pastry Puffs, 67
Shortcut Brunswick Stew, 53
Shrimp in Pastry Puffs, 67

Side Dishes (*see also* **Vegetables**)
Bulgur with Basil and Walnuts, 80
Vegetable Couscous, 79
Skillet Black-Eyed Peas 'n' Rice, 12
Smoked Turkey Bean Soup, 24
Souper Chicken Tetrazzini, 35
Souper-Easy Cheese Dip, 90

Soups and Stews
Broccoli Fish Chowder, 29
Chicken 'n' Shrimp Gumbo, 24
Cincinnati Chili, 41
Country Ham 'n' Potato Soup, 25
Creamy Shrimp Bisque, 20
Curried Chicken Vegetable Chowder,
30
Double Clam Chowder, 85
Down-Home Vegetable Chowder, 85
Easy Creole Soup, 36
Garden-Style Vegetable Bisque, 36
German-Style Pork Stew, 62
Ham Barley Soup, 61
Hearty Sausage 'n' Cabbage Soup, 49
Hint-of-Mint Pea Soup, 82
Knockwurst Potato Chowder, 22
Macaroni Ratatouille Soup, 60
Meatball 'n' Green Bean Soup, 67
Nacho Pork Chili, 62
Pepperoni Pizza Soup, 18
Philadelphia Cheesesteak Soup, 25
Quick Gazpacho, 82
Shortcut Brunswick Stew, 53
Smoked Turkey Bean Soup, 24
South-of-the-Border Onion Soup, 84
Southwest Potato Soup, 85
Speedy Spicy Chili, 13
Spicy Bean Soup, 22
Summer Garden Soup, 80
Tuna-Tortellini Soup, 20
Watercress Potato Soup, 84
Winter Lamb Stew, 64
South-of-the-Border Onion Soup, 84

Southwest Mac and Beef, 42
Southwest Potato Soup, 85
Speedy Spicy Chili, 13
Spicy Bean Soup, 22
Spicy Broccoli Beef, 12
Spicy Potatoes Olé, 72
Spinach Meat Loaves, Zesty, 64
Squash 'n' Macaroni in Spicy Cheese
Sauce, 73
Summer Garden Soup, 80
Szechuan Shredded Pork, 13

Taco Salad, 44
Tamale Pie, 60
Tortilla Cups, 10
Tuna-Tortellini Soup, 20

Turkey (*see also* **Chicken**)
Easy Turkey Salad, 18
Smoked Turkey Bean Soup, 24
Turkey-Vegetable Pot Pie, 51
Vegetable Couscous, 79

Vegetables
Broccoli Bake, 74
Broccoli-Rice Casserole, 73
Bulgur with Basil and Walnuts, 80
Cheese-Sauced Summer Vegetables,
78
Curried Peanut Rice, 78
Curry-Sauced Cauliflower, 70
Down-Home Vegetable Chowder, 85
Double Clam Chowder, 85
Gingered Vegetables, 69
Hint-of-Mint Pea Soup, 82
Mixed Vegetable Pilaf, 76
Mushrooms in Garlic-Herb Sauce, 76
Peas and Carrots in Thyme Sauce,
74
Potato Skin Nachos, 89
Quick Gazpacho, 82
Quick Rice and Beans, 72
Savory Parslied Rice, 79
South-of-the-Border Onion Soup, 84
Southwest Potato Soup, 85
Spicy Potatoes Olé, 72
Squash 'n' Macaroni in Spicy Cheese
Sauce, 73
Summer Garden Soup, 80
Vegetable Couscous, 79
Vegetables in Two Cheese-Beer
Sauce, 70
Watercress Potato Soup, 84

Watercress Potato Soup, 84
Winter Lamb Stew, 64